BEST VERSION EVER

BEST VERSION EVER

DISCOVER THE MAGIC OF BECOMING EXTRAORDINARY

JOSH PAINTER

LIONCREST
PUBLISHING

BEST VERSION EVER
Discover the MAGIC of Becoming Extraordinary

FIRST EDITION

ISBN   978-1-5445-3788-7 *Hardcover*
       978-1-5445-3787-0 *Paperback*
       978-1-5445-3789-4 *Ebook*

To your eighteen-year-old and eighty-year-old self. May you make them both proud.

CONTENTS

INTRODUCTION

There's something very depressing about watching grown men live their lives in cages, but five years into working as a corrections officer at a county jail, I realized my life had become a prison of its own.

I remember driving to work, a miserable two-hour commute each way, listening to the words of Pearl Jam's "Sleight of Hand." Leaving the house at 4 a.m., the sun wasn't even out, and I knew when I left work at 7 p.m. that the sun would be long gone. Like the man in the song, I was waking up just to pour myself into a uniform. I wondered what I was doing with my life.

I was seventeen when my girlfriend got pregnant. I finished high school early, got married, and got a "real job" because I thought that was what you were supposed to do. I rented apartments, bought a house, took on debt, and got credit cards because I thought that was what you were supposed to do. I was a young guy trying to support a family without a thought about doing something I'd really love. I was living the life I thought others expected of me, and pursuing the "success" we're taught to want.

Many of us spend our lives on autopilot: we work eight hours a day at jobs we hate. We pay bills and buy things we don't need. We live in homes or cities that we don't love. We stay in unhealthy relationships. We eat and drink things that make us fat and sick. We scroll social media mindlessly. We're so complacent, afraid of risk, or concerned about disappointing others that we ignore the dreams we want to pursue.

Most people live that life because it's scary not to. Most people default to whatever is comfortable because it's not fun to rock the boat. Going against what others expect from you *is* uncomfortable—it may be the scariest thing you'll ever do—so the pain of staying the same *has* to become greater than the pain of changing.

Consider this: What would you do if you had no limitations? What would you do if you had no uncertainty about the outcome? What would it take, and who would you need to become to do those things right now?

Making changes means taking risks, but doing nothing and not changing carries the risk that you'll die having never actually lived.

I had never wanted to be average. Growing up, I always had a sense that there was more to life and that I was destined to do great things. I always wondered why some people I knew seemed okay with settling for mediocrity in their lives. Yet there I was doing the same thing.

It's been said that the two best days of your life are the day you were born and the day you discover why. Turning thirty was my turning point. I thought, *If I don't do something different with my life, then before I know it, I'm going to wake up at forty, and nothing will have changed. Ten more years of living someone else's life, under someone else's rules.* My thirtieth birthday was the day I figured out my why, even if I couldn't yet articulate it.

I didn't want to be like Bronnie Ware's dying patients, who commonly said, as described in her book *The Top Five Regrets of the Dying*, "I wish I'd had the courage to live a life true to myself, not the life others expected of me."

When I was twenty-six, I realized I was not where I wanted to be, so I left the corrections officer job to pursue mortgage loans. But it wasn't until I was thirty that I started making changes in my life. That's when I went all in on finding out what *my* Best Version Ever was.

Since then, I've built a real estate company that has sold over one billion dollars worth of homes and ranks in the Top 10 in sales in California. I sold the company at a seven-figure valuation in the middle of a pandemic, and I now lead and coach hundreds of goal achievers all over the country.

We tend to miss out on the present because we're obsessed with building the future others expect of us. If life is a song, the tendency to build our lives for some distant future we may never see is like looking forward to that last note…meanwhile, we miss the whole point: we're supposed to be dancing while the music plays.

Success is being true to ourselves, continually becoming our

Best Version Ever, whatever that looks like. For some, this could be changing careers, focusing on health, setting relationship boundaries, or being a better parent. For some, this could be volunteering, traveling, and crossing off bucket list items. And for others, this could be as simple as surfing every day after work.

I've learned that true success, for me, is becoming my Best Version Ever in all aspects of my life. I remarried and developed great relationships with my grown kids, friends, and family. I have achieved many personal goals, including traveling regularly, playing music, and losing the fifty pounds I gained as a jail guard. I have even made a lasting impact on the world by founding a charity organization that has raised over $200,000 in the last few years.

On this journey to becoming my Best Version Ever, I studied the world's best goal achievers to learn strategies for achievement. I joined several groups, went to conferences, and even did the Tony Robbins thing, where we all walked across burning coals in a parking lot at 1 a.m. But I noticed these events tended to have the same outcome: I was motivated for a day or two before falling back into my old routines. I wanted to be my Best Version Ever for life, not for a few days.

I studied the events themselves to discover why they didn't bring lasting change, and I realized that most leave you with information overload. You write down all these ideas in a journal, and you get home and implement nothing. There's no plan of action or community to fall back on.

I decided to take matters into my own hands and create the

event I wished I could've attended when starting to become my Best Version Ever. I compiled my notes from all of the conferences I attended. I read a stack of personal development books, highlighting key points and writing all over the margins. I watched hundreds of hours of videos, taking pages and pages of handwritten notes. Then, after months of prep, I decided to try out my own version of a goal-setting event.

I invited a small group to my house, but I didn't expect what happened next. There were vulnerable conversations, massive goals, laughter, crying, and big hugs. Then, months later, the messages started coming in from the members of that first group:

"I lost fifteen pounds!"

"I bought my first house!"

"I doubled my income and crushed my sales goals!"

"I raced motocross for the first time in years, and won!"

Nothing I've ever done has had the same impact on me and those around me as this event, which has since been opened to the public. So now, I've created a MAGIC formula to help you become *your* Best Version Ever.

Every successful person has a turning point, the moment they decide they're not going to live a mediocre life anymore. By holding this book, you may be making that decision now.

In this book, you will learn:

- **Mindset:** How to shift your thinking from negative to positive so you will be open to new possibilities.
- **Aim:** How to identify and narrow down the goals you want to pursue.
- **Gameplan:** How to create a schedule that allows you to gain momentum toward short- and long-term goals.
- **Immersion:** How to promote learning and take action through commitment, continuous learning, and mentorship.
- **Consistency:** How to develop lifelong habits that will make your changes sustainable.

In the final chapter, **Becoming**, you will also learn how to put these concepts together, get back on track when you fall off, stay true to yourself, and give back to others.

This book is meant to be a lifelong roadmap filled with tips and actions to get you started on the journey. Feel free to highlight and underline, write in the margins, and come back to it again and again. Books aren't meant to look brand new, so make this one yours.

Just to clarify—this book is not strictly about achieving your goals. While that's an aspect, becoming your Best Version Ever is an ongoing process. Your Best Version Ever today may not be the same as your Best Version Ever in a few years. To live a life without regrets, we need to be constantly evaluating and improving.

This is also not a five hundred-page scientific textbook detailing health or business advice. Things that were "true" one hundred years ago are laughable now, and vice versa, so you do you. From time to time, I'll touch on these topics with tips that have helped me along the way, but we all need to walk our own path. Question everything, and find what works for you.

This book is the most current version of my "truth," my Best Version Ever, and I hope it helps you find yours. Because as long as we're alive and the song is playing, we should be dancing.

CHAPTER I

MINDSET

It was like playing debit card roulette: I pulled up to the gas pump, put in my last $60, filled up my tank, and raced to the ATM. I withdrew $60 before the charge for the gas went through because I needed that money to show some houses to a buyer—and to buy food.

Only a few months before, I had been a mortgage loan officer when the real estate market suddenly tanked. It was 2008, and I didn't have the experience or the mindset to survive the largest financial meltdown of my lifetime. Before I knew it, I had lost my house to foreclosure, even after borrowing $10,000 from my parents to try to hold onto it. I then filed for bankruptcy and completed my trifecta of bad credit by getting a divorce.

Now living in a two-bedroom apartment that cost $600 a month, I was sleeping on the couch so my son and daughter could each have a room when I had them. Since loans were taking forever to close at the time, I was already three months behind on rent.

I called my parents, saying, "I only need another $2,000. I'm not going to ask you for money again. I'm almost there." Though they didn't believe me, they sent the money.

Unsure about the future, I remembered the advice my mentor, Tony, had given me when I was starting out in the mortgage business. "Look, today, someone is getting married. Someone is being born. Someone is passing away. Someone is graduating college. Someone is being promoted. Someone is being transferred. Someone is getting divorced. There will *always* be people who need to buy a house and people who need to sell a house. That will *never* change."

Tony had decades of experience, and his advice soon proved true: a loan I had worked on for months finally closed, and I earned about $400 for my hard work. I called the real estate agent to congratulate her, and she said something I'll never forget: "Oh, this wasn't really a big deal for me. I only made $4,000."

That day, my mindset changed. I decided I would commit to real estate—as an agent.

I already had my real estate license and had spent the last three years working closely with real estate agents, so I knew what it took to succeed. I knew that there was nothing that I couldn't learn and achieve if I just put in enough effort and time. I knew that if others were successful in this business, I could be too. I truly believed that anything I saw someone else do was proof I could do the same thing.

With this newfound determination, I drove to a local real estate brokerage, walked in, and asked, "Hey, how do I sign up?" I bought twelve open house signs the next day, found an empty bank-owned home for sale, and put the signs up. People started walking in, and I even wrote an offer on the house.

That offer didn't get accepted, but I remember thinking, *If I can do this forty hours a week, there is no way I won't sell one house a month.*

I worked eight hours a day, hosting open houses, publishing online ads, showing homes, mailing letters to everyone I knew, and dropping flyers at apartment buildings. Within three months, I had sold a few houses. I had even caught up on my rent.

Once I changed my mindset, everything changed. And the best part? On Mother's Day, almost a year later, I gave my mom a check for $12,000.

When you shift from a negative to a positive mindset and take some time to reflect, you can learn quickly from your mistakes, quit repeating them, let go of the baggage in your life, appreciate where you are, and determine what you want to do next.

POSITIVE THINKING

In 1979, researchers had a group of elderly men live for a week in an environment modeled after 1959, with vintage clothing, a black-and-white TV, old radios, and newspapers. They were supposed to act like it was 1959 and experience the world through fifty-five-year-old eyes. Photos of their younger selves surrounded them, and they discussed events from the fifties as if they were currently happening. They even played a football game on the front lawn on the last day of the study.

A week later, researchers tested the group, and nearly everyone had improved their strength, posture, memory, hearing, and vision. In fact, a few people unaware of the study looked at the before and after photos of the men and guessed that those in the "after" photos were about two years younger than the ones in the "before."

How does this study relate to you becoming your Best Version Ever?

By changing their mindsets, those men improved both mentally and physically. Like them, you are a consciousness observing your thoughts, and these thoughts affect what you experience, how you feel, and who you become.

You are always talking to yourself. It never stops. The voice in your head is constantly narrating, making observations and judgments about the outside world. Our thoughts are rooted in our past experiences and can either work for us or against us, depending on how we choose to use them.

We become what we focus on, so it is helpful to direct your thoughts toward the positive. When you create an optimistic outlook on life, you can see what is possible.

Say you go car shopping and decide you want a black Honda Civic. As soon as you've developed the mindset that you want that car, you will start to notice black Honda Civics everywhere you go. Now here's the thing: they were always there. You never saw them because your mind wasn't primed to look for them.

When we consume fear-based media, we start to believe that the world is dangerous and begin worrying about more and more threats. Suddenly a petty crime in the neighborhood becomes evidence that society is deteriorating. Like the black Honda Civic, the petty crime has always been there; you're just paying more attention and noticing it daily.

If you instead prime your mind to see the positive through gratitude and affirmations, you can improve your mental and physical health.

GRATITUDE

Every time I'm on a plane, I look out the window at all the tiny houses below, thinking about how each one has people inside who have their own problems and dreams. It reminds me how big the world is, how insignificant my problems are, and how fortunate I am to live where and when I do.

Sometimes all we need to feel grateful is some perspective on the world: our worst day might be someone else's best day ever. While others have to walk miles for water, we have little rivers in our bathrooms and kitchens that we can turn on whenever we want. While others live on the streets or in poverty, we take showers in heated tropical waterfalls. The water in our toilets is cleaner than the drinking water in some countries.

Other times, we need some perspective on our own lives. For instance, at my event, we list out all the things in life we can and can't control, and it's always illuminating because it shows how we can shift our mindset. You might naturally be frustrated about traffic, but you can instead say to yourself, *I'm lucky to be alive and able to drive a car today.*

We may not be able to control the weather, the economy, taxes, or the actions of others, but we can control how we prepare and react. As my friend says, "There's no such thing as bad weather, just bad wardrobes and bad planning."

Sometimes even the most detailed plans and wardrobe aren't enough to prevent frustration due to circumstances beyond our control. It's easy to lose sight of the good things and slip back into negative thinking. To keep things in perspective and focus on the abundance around me, I keep a running list of things I'm grateful for every year.

For instance, after a challenging year I had recently, it would have been understandable to become depressed. But when I looked back at my gratitude list, I was reminded that in the same year, I sold a business, traveled with friends, moved to the beach, and got back into surfing. In addition, my wife got her marriage and family therapist license, my son finished his time in the Navy, and my daughter graduated college.

Some people keep a gratitude journal on their desk or beside their bed and write down a few things they're grateful for each day. Gratitude then becomes a habit that supports your mindset shift.

The Neuroscience of Gratitude

If you focus on what you don't have, you will never have enough; you will always be in a deficit state. Our negativity bias is a good thing—we're wired to notice threats in our environment, which has kept us alive since the beginning of humanity—but the fear that results can hold you back from becoming your Best Version Ever. To avoid the physical and mental consequences of negativity bias, it's important to intentionally practice gratitude.

Our lives are shaped by what we consume, whether it's food, music, television, news, or social media. If we feed our mind negative images, for instance, that's all we'll ever see and all we'll ever experience.

Fortunately, we can create new neural pathways, priming our brains to create memories and learn new behaviors. This concept is called neuroplasticity. In other words, when we use gratitude to focus on the positive things in our lives, our attention is naturally drawn to the resources and opportunities we *do* have.

Gratitude opens our eyes to the good in life, making the present moment more meaningful. This practice activates the parts of the brain involved in reward, morality, social bonding, and empathy. In addition, important chemicals like dopamine, serotonin, and oxytocin are released. All of these neurological factors contribute to feelings of connectedness and happiness.

Incremental Growth

In this age of lightning-fast internet speeds and same-day delivery services, we've become impatient with anything less than instant gratification. Because social media is like a public diary, we're tempted to only share what's going well. We want our lives to look like a never-ending highlight reel.

However, our lives are made up of tiny habits and decisions, many of which can seem inconsequential at the time. Consistent, incremental daily improvements can lead to massive gains over time, yet most of us don't have the commitment it takes to strive for these barely noticeable daily improvements.

For instance, I do a few daily things, such as reading, journaling, and exercising. While it doesn't always seem like much is happening, these habits allow me to make continual progress toward the positive mindset and healthy lifestyle I strive to maintain.

It goes the opposite way, too: eating an extra slice of pizza or grabbing candy at the store might not seem like a big deal at the moment, but the average person over thirty gains approximately two pounds per year. This number may seem trivial, but next thing you know, ten years have gone by, and you've gained twenty pounds—not all at once, but as a result of poor decisions every day.

What does this have to do with your positive mindset? If you choose to practice gratitude daily, the continual release of various happiness chemicals in your brain will make that feeling your default. As a result, you will biologically shift your mindset from negative to positive.

We can't control everything that happens to us, but we always have the power to decide how we respond. Life is seldom about what happens and almost entirely about how we react, and as soon as we take responsibility for our own happiness, everything changes. We choose the meaning that we attach to events and whether to be grateful for all that happens in our lives.

Gratitude builds on itself, so keep practicing. Consistency is key.

TAKE ACTION

I've included "Take Action" sections throughout the book with exercises proven to help you become your Best Version Ever. You can use blank paper or a journal for all activities. You may also download my Best Version Ever Workbook with all of the action items at BestVersionEver.com

During these exercises, you may find it helpful to go out in nature or find a quiet spot at home where you can spend some time journaling without distractions or interruptions. I like to silence my notifications and put on some calming music. Find what works for you, and take action.

* * *

On one side of a piece of paper, list all the things you can control. On the other side, list all the things you can't control. Consider how you could proactively respond to the things you can control and positively react to the things you can't.

Then write down five things that you are grateful for. For instance:

- Five people:
- Five things about my relationship or friendships:
- Five things about my community and where I live:
- Five things about my work:
- Five more things I am grateful for:

Go through your photos, calendar, and social media to identify all your wins over the last year or few years. Then make a Top 10 list and celebrate the abundance in your life.

AFFIRMATIONS

Leveraging the same concept of neuroplasticity that we talked about with gratitude, you can write the script for your life with affirmations. Where you can use gratitude to appreciate the gifts of the present, you can use affirmations to feel encouraged rather than intimidated by future possibilities.

Your mind wants to believe what you tell it, so if you tell yourself that you're becoming an attentive partner, an amazing parent, or even an expert drummer, you'll eventually start to see that it's possible and believe that it's true. Consider: who do I want to become? Then tell yourself that you are on your way there.

Affirmations aren't wishful or magical thinking. Contrary to what many believe, affirmations don't work if there's no truth behind them. For example, you can't say, "I am healthy" if you're not and expect to believe it because your brain knows when you're lying. Instead, you could say, "I am becoming healthy," which would likely give you the confidence to begin making healthier lifestyle choices.

Furthermore, you can't manifest the life you want without taking action. For example, you can't say, "I am a millionaire," and expect to win a large jackpot because the lottery isn't something you can control. Instead, you could say, "I am creating wealth for myself and my family," which would make it more likely that you could see potentially lucrative opportunities in your life.

Affirmations have gotten a bad rap, usually because they are misunderstood. It's become a joke that if you stare at yourself in a mirror and repeat these affirming statements as loud as possible, your life will magically change. But if you've ever told yourself "You've got this" before facing a difficult situation, you've used affirmations without realizing it.

Written and spoken affirmations are a tool to gradually change to more positive thinking and reflect on who you want to become, but you don't have to make them cheesy or shout them while staring at yourself. I like to write a few down in a journal while speaking to myself; you have to find a practice that works for you.

TAKE ACTION

Write three positive affirmations beginning with "I am..."

Instead of writing them as fast as you can, think about the abundance surrounding you. Say these to yourself as you write. Add some emotion, and feel that these are future possibilities.

REFLECTION

1 in 400 trillion. Maybe even 1 in 400 quadrillion. The answer varies based on who you ask, but one thing everyone seems to agree on: basically zero.

Those are the odds that you would be born.

Your parents had to meet at the exact moment they did. If one of them happened to be running thirty minutes late, they might never have met. They had to like each other enough to want to keep seeing each other, above and beyond all the other men and women they met along the way.

Your mother was born with around 100,000 eggs but had only one available every month. Your father, during his reproductive years, had trillions of sperm. Despite all of the potential combinations, you are one egg and one sperm in one moment in time.

You were competing against several hundred million racers, and you alone crossed the finish line. The odds were basically zero, but you won the first race you ever entered.

Let's take this further: think about your grandparents meeting, their parents meeting, and keep going up your family tree. When you think about the odds, it's clear that your birth and life are a miracle. So what will you do with this opportunity?

From an early age, we start asking "What is the purpose of my life?" as if we're expecting an answer. At the same time, life asks us the same question in return. Your life has infinite potential—what will you do with it?

Your life's purpose is to become your Best Version Ever, and you constantly determine what that looks like. Your Best Version Ever isn't a place you ever reach or a finish line you ever cross; it's a continually evolving state. You are always becoming.

How you define your Best Version Ever is entirely up to you. But to decide who you will become, you must first reflect on who you are.

INQUIRY

The desire to better understand who we are makes us human. Unlike other creatures, we can be mesmerized by a sunset, overwhelmed by art, or moved to tears by a song. We can contemplate our actions, thoughts, and feelings, as well as feel empathy for others.

Self-awareness is something humans have always worked on and strived for. In fact, a prominent Greek inscription carved into the Temple of Apollo at Delphi says, "Know thyself." We want to know ourselves: what we want, where we belong in the world, and how we affect others.

Inquiry is all about asking questions to get to know yourself, and there are many ways you can do this. For instance, you could identify how you experience and express love using Gary Chapman's *The Five Love Languages*, determine your attachment style using Amir Levine and Rachel S. F. Heller's *Attached*, or even study general psychology. In addition, you could ask yourself questions that will open your eyes to possibilities, such as "What is going well for me right now?" or "When was I at my best?"

You will grow in any area of persistent inquiry, so by asking questions, you can begin to imagine and build a future based on your core strengths and values. You can also use inquiry to question your beliefs. Who are you? Why are you? Did you choose your beliefs, or were they planted by your parents, teachers, friends, celebrities, and society?

When we don't reflect, we go through life without pausing to consider how things are going. Instead, we keep doing what we've always done, like remaining in unhealthy relationships or jobs we don't enjoy, even when they're not working out.

Questioning your actions, thoughts, ideas, and beliefs enables you to get a better look at your life. You can determine if you're heading in the right direction and adjust as needed. You can clarify your thinking and determine what matters regarding your past experiences and future potential.

To become your Best Version Ever, you have to understand how you think, how those thoughts and actions have brought you to this present moment, and how they can help you become more. This is an ongoing process, since there is always something new to learn about ourselves, but knowing where you're at will help you decide and commit to where you're going.

TAKE ACTION

The following questions are meant to open your mind to the strengths, gifts, and possibilities all around you.

Consider why becoming your Best Version Ever at this moment is meaningful to you right now.

Q. How could choosing to become your Best Version Ever right now be a significant and fulfilling experience for you? In what ways does becoming your Best Version Ever benefit family, friends, and the world around you?

Think of times in your life when you've been at your best and shown up as the best version of yourself to others.

Q. How did you use your strengths on these occasions? What strengths do you hope to see more of in the future?

Take a moment to appreciate the connections, opportunities, and talents you have in your life.

Q. In what ways are you most grateful for your life? What do you like most about yourself and the world around you?

Visualize yourself becoming your Best Version Ever and doing so in a way that gives you a deep sense of accomplishment, significance, and fulfillment.

Q. What would happen if you achieved everything you set out to do? What would this feel like for you?

Imagine becoming the person you've always dreamed of being.

Q. What would you like to see yourself achieving in the future?

Consider your life's purpose and the vision you hold for the future.

Q. In what ways can you set intentions right now to help you become your Best Version Ever?

Adapted from Jon Berghoff's XCHANGE Approach, a method for designing questions and conversations that unlock potential in groups and individuals.

MEDITATION

Admittedly, I still have difficulty meditating, so generally when I practice, I use a meditation app to keep myself focused. One of my favorite things to do when I want to meditate is use a sensory deprivation float tank.

The first tank was designed in 1954 by John C. Lilly, an American physician and neuroscientist who wanted to study the origins of consciousness. These tanks are filled with ~800 pounds of Epsom salt in a foot of water so that you can float weightlessly; the water is heated to your body temperature, and each tank is situated in a small, pitch black, soundproof room so that you feel cut off from all external stimuli. With your senses removed, you can think without distraction.

But why meditate at all? You can increase your mental clarity by focusing your attention on your breath, an object, or even a thought. Meditation is a state of being, where you just are, and some of the most brilliant people in history have used one form or another to help them become extraordinary.

How can meditation shift your mindset and help you become your Best Version Ever? By observing your thoughts, you realize that your thoughts do not define you. As you become more aware of what you are thinking, you can focus more on what you want to give attention to, and you can start to let go of negative thinking that doesn't serve you.

Research shows that meditation lowers cortisol, the hormone that regulates our fear and stress responses, while improving the part of the brain that governs our higher-order functions. As a result, meditation can reduce inflammation, blood pressure, anger, anxiety, and depression; it can improve concentration, productivity, creativity, mood, and sleep.

Whether you sit in silence, pray, do yoga, or even float weightlessly in a tank of salt water, dedicating time to meditate daily can do wonders for your mental and physical health. It's not always easy; it can be challenging to tune things out, to stay in the present moment rather than thinking about the past or the future. As with any other skill, it takes practice, but meditation can help you focus and live in the present moment.

TAKE ACTION

Close your eyes and notice everything that you sense. Am I seeing something? Am I hearing something? Am I feeling something? It never fails when I meditate that I get itchy. Allow yourself to sense these things, and then let them go.

There's a misconception that you're not supposed to think during meditation. Quiet your mind, and observe your thoughts without judgment.

Your mind will wander, and that's okay. Once you realize you're distracted, acknowledge your thoughts and let them go, like a cloud moving in the sky. Then bring your focus back to your breath.

RISK-TAKING

In 1971, Fred Smith started the FedEx delivery company based on an idea he wrote about in a term paper while majoring in economics at Yale in 1962 called "Overnight Delivery Service in a Computer Information Age." In that paper, he described the benefits of changing shipping strategies for companies so that they could deliver items overnight, which at the time had never been done.

FedEx nearly went bankrupt three years after it began, as fuel costs soared rapidly. The company was losing over $1 million every month, and no one was willing to provide further investment or loans to the company.

When the company's bank account balance dwindled to $5,000 after Smith's final pitch for more funding was rejected by General Dynamics, Smith knew they wouldn't be able to fuel their delivery planes the following Monday.

Rather than returning home, Smith took the company's last $5,000 and flew to Las Vegas to play Black Jack that weekend. On Monday, to the surprise of everyone in the company, FedEx was sitting on $27,000 in its bank account. Smith had turned $5,000 into $27,000 in Black Jack winnings, which was just enough to cover the fuel for their planes so they could continue operating for another week.

When asked about taking a risk with what little money the

company had left, Smith shrugged his shoulders and replied, "What difference does it make? Without the funds for the fuel companies, we couldn't have flown anyway."

All it took was a few more days. FedEx made its first profit of $3.6 million in 1976 after raising $11 million from investors to keep the company afloat, and today, the company is worth over $50 billion.

Life is nothing more than a series of calculated risks. Risk is inherent in everything we do, and a positive outcome is never guaranteed, so we must know which risks are worth taking to become our Best Version Ever. To do this, we must acknowledge how the spotlight effect, imposter syndrome, and loss aversion can prevent us from taking any risks at all.

Spotlight Effect

There is this dichotomy where, on the one hand, we are the star of our own life's movie, and on the other, we're merely supporting characters in everyone else's. Because we're all wrapped up in our own spotlight effect, we overestimate how much others notice our appearance or behavior.

For example, when a group photo is taken, the first thing we all see is ourselves. If we don't like how we look in a picture, if our hair is out of place or if we don't smile the way we want to, it ruins the photo for us—even though no one else notices, let alone cares about, that slight imperfection. We're all worried about our own shortcomings.

Despite this spotlight effect, many people don't take risks because they fear rejection. The truth is, someone might reject you in the moment, but they're not thinking about you afterward; they've moved on with their own worries and wishes. We never want to take anything personally because we don't know what someone else is going through, and often, it's not really about you anyway. If someone makes fun of you or doesn't like what you're doing…that is their experience. It only affects your experience if you allow it to.

It can be freeing to realize that most people don't care about or even notice your minor flaws because they are so focused on their own. Perhaps it opens you up to trying new things you've put off doing out of fear of what others would think about you.

Imposter Syndrome

Often we fear that we will mess up and someone will find out we're unqualified, so we hesitate to take risks. But this fear of failure is paralyzing.

"Better safe than sorry" is a dream killer. If you assume you will fail, you'll never try, and if you never try, you'll miss out on great opportunities. You'll never become your Best Version Ever.

The truth is, you *can* fail when you try something new. You can study and consume info all you want, but nothing will teach you like doing it. You've heard the saying, "Fake it until you make it"—that is to say, jump in and go for it. Learn as you go. Fail as you go. You can reframe your mindset to consider failure as an opportunity to improve your skills rather than as a risk you're not going to take.

Once I auditioned for a band that had lost their drummer nine days before a show. I'd been drumming for about a year, and they were leagues ahead of me as musicians, so I had no business being there. I felt like an imposter, but I auditioned anyway, telling the band I'd learn their forty songs in nine days so they wouldn't have to cancel the show.

I practiced for six to eight hours a day and learned the basics of those forty songs, but I kept making noticeable mistakes. I played the show but got fired from the band after a few months. Still, I learned so much from the experience, from the dynamics of playing quieter in smaller spaces, to adding nuance instead of playing songs note-for-note.

When trying something new, quantity leads to quality; it's not the other way around. You can't read, watch, listen, and study forever—at some point, you just do. Don't let your research become a form of procrastination. Minutes lead to hours, which lead to days, which lead to weeks. Each failure is a necessary part of your eventual success. It's painful, but we must go through it to reach our goals, and we must not fear that the rejection or failure we experience will lead to loss.

Loss Aversion

Suppose you want to get a promotion at work, but you are afraid of being rejected by your boss. You fear failing in this endeavor, but your resulting inaction brings on the loss since you never asked for what you want. As a result, you end up working your same old job while slowly growing to resent the person who earned your desired promotion.

There is a human tendency to prefer to avoid losses over similar gains because, for most people, losing hurts more than gaining feels good. For instance, the pain of losing $1,000 can feel worse than finding or winning $1,000. Insurance is another example: we love security, so we prefer to pay a small amount regularly to protect us from the unlikely loss of large amounts in a catastrophic future event.

Loss aversion gets even stronger when the stakes are higher. For instance, as a real estate agent, I sometimes had clients think that because they added $100,000 in upgrades to their home, it must be worth $100,000 more, but that's not how the real estate market works. As a result, these clients would try—and fail—to sell their home for more than it was worth to avoid perceived loss.

While loss aversion, like negativity bias, can be beneficial, it can also be driven by emotions rather than logic, which can lead to poor decisions. Sometimes, when faced with a significant life change, people will cling to their comfort zone, even if that's the life others expect of them. Changing may feel like a loss of identity, and the "loss" of everything they know may feel greater than the potential gain of a "new" them.

Whether we avoid risk because we fear rejection, failure, or loss, it's essential to ask, "Will this matter in five years?"

I try to remind myself that everything is temporary—the good and the bad. So when something sets me back for a few days, weeks, months, or even a whole year, I know eventually it will no longer be a thought to me. I'm not currently worrying about things from five years ago; in five years, I won't be worrying about what's happening today.

When you reflect on what's holding you back from taking risks, consider whether those fears will matter in five years. Chances are they won't, so don't let today's hesitation hold you back from pursuing tomorrow's Best Version Ever.

TAKE ACTION

Let's reframe. If you're facing a decision that could be driven by fear of loss, try focusing on the potential outcome and upside of the situation.

Now let's play "Worst Case Scenario." Imagine the worst thing that could happen if you made that same decision. Even if the worst case scenario played out, then what? How would you react? Sometimes imagining the worst possible outcome can put things in perspective and help determine if taking action is worth it.

MOVING FORWARD

Can you name five to ten things about your great-great-grandparents? How about one? Most people can't. Occasionally when I ask this, someone will name a handful of things—and it's because they were on a genealogy website the day before.

Your great-great-grandparents passed away less than one hundred years ago. Like them, we will be gone and forgotten within one hundred years, yet we go about life on autopilot.

Your legacy isn't about having your name on a building one hundred years from now; we shouldn't spend our lives focused on being remembered by people we will never even meet. How you make people feel in the present moment is how the world will remember you. That is your legacy.

As you read this book, this is the youngest you will ever be. You are never too old to take massive action and live the life you dream about. If not now, then when?

CHAPTER 2

AIM

I showed up at the office in my best Ross Dress For Less threads with no clue what to expect. A couple of days beforehand, my office manager had texted me, with no context, "Do you want to work with some investors in San Diego?"

I had so many questions on my mind. *What kind of investors? Flips? Rentals? Where in San Diego? What price range?* Most people would've probably started asking away, but I'd just typed, "Yes."

At the last minute, the office manager texted again: "I'm not going to be able to meet them, but you'll be fine." Great—I was on my own.

During the meeting, sitting around a conference room table, the investors said they had raised enough funds to buy a few houses, and down the road, they wanted to buy and flip two houses per month consistently. It would be a success if they could flip twenty-four houses per year.

They needed an agent to help them navigate the auction process, value homes, and manage the renovation process. They especially wanted an agent who could help them find someone to bid on their homes at the auctions.

Of course, I told them I could do all of that, and I explained what some of the processes would look like. I even came up with a potential scenario for how we could do the bidding at the auction. I had no clue what I was talking about, but I must have convinced them, because at the end of the meeting, they asked me to send them a proposal.

A proposal? I thought. *What does that mean? Didn't I just propose everything to them?*

When I got home, I searched "Proposal Template" and downloaded a Word document, filling it in with my information and what I believed I would be doing for them. I sent it that evening and waited. And waited.

I waited the entire weekend. Then, on Monday morning, I received a call.

"We like your proposal. We've already bought one house at auction. Why don't you meet us at the house tomorrow at 9 a.m. and bring the contractor you usually work with?"

Shit. I didn't even know any contractors. I must have acted like I did in the meeting.

I called a bunch of agents I knew, asking for contractor recommendations, and the name Greg came up more than once.

I called him, saying, "Look, I don't know you, but I may have a pretty big opportunity for both of us." I asked if he could meet me half an hour before everyone else so we could "bro out." We would get to know each other and act like we'd worked together for a while already.

Greg, fortunately, was all in.

The following day, I met him for the first time. Greg and I got to know each other and came up with a strategy: while we walked the house with the investors, he would answer any renovation-related questions, and I would answer any real estate and market-related questions. We wouldn't talk over each other, and things would flow.

When the walk-through ended that morning, one of the investors said, "We are ready to list with an agent soon. We will call you and let you know."

I got in my car, hopes high. During the past few days, I'd had no idea what I was doing, but I made it my aim to become the best real estate agent I could be, and my mindset was primed to look for relevant opportunities.

Minutes later, my phone rang. I could see it was the investor's number. I looked in my rearview mirror and saw him, phone to ear, in his car.

"We'd like to work with you. Send over the contract."

Once we aligned our goals, we went on to sell more than twenty-four houses a year. In fact, at the height of our partnership, I managed sixty homes at a time, and I built a team of eight drivers to scout the properties, three assistants, and two auction bidders. One year, I sold 165 homes, and I ended up selling nearly four hundred houses in total for the investors.

Once your mindset is primed for becoming your Best Version Ever, you can begin determining your overall aim and setting the goals that will help you along the way.

GETTING STARTED

Jim Carrey always knew he was destined to become famous, even as a broke young actor. During an interview, he described the visualization practice he used to manifest his goals. He would park on Mulholland Drive and stare at the city lights below, imagining the world's possibilities.

He says, "I would visualize things coming to me that I wanted. I had nothing at that time, but it just made me feel better. I would drive home and think, 'Well, I do have these things. They're out there; I just don't have ahold of them yet.'"

During his struggles, he wrote himself a check for ten million dollars. In the memo, it said, "For acting services rendered." He gave himself three years, dating it "Thanksgiving 1995," and placed the check in his wallet, where it deteriorated over the years.

Just short of the three-year mark, he found out he would make ten million dollars starring in the movie *Dumb & Dumber*. When his father died, Jim put the check he had written to himself into his dad's pocket, which was buried with him.

As you prepare yourself to pursue the goals you set, you can use visualization to fully imagine what you want to achieve in the future as if it has already happened. Where affirmations allow you to write the script for your life, visualization is watching that script play out.

AFTERTHOUGHTS

If you're a pessimist, always anticipating and planning for the worst-case scenario, you may unconsciously take actions that attract negative things into your life. You're visualizing a negative outcome and making it happen.

Visualize what you *want*, not what you *expect*, and then use your positive mindset to avoid a self-fulfilling prophecy.

VISUALIZATION

As discussed in Chapter 1, neuroplasticity refers to how learning something new leaves an impression on your brain. This concept explains why repeating or practicing a task more often will etch it more solidly in your memory, making it easier to recall.

Research shows that if you visualize a concept repeatedly, your brain begins to react as if it were really happening. One study even showed that visualizing an exercise activates the same brain regions as performing it physically, which is why many athletes use visualization as a walk-through before a big game. Your brain can essentially train your body on what to do.

Having used visualization before a big presentation, before playing sports, and even before performing in a band on stage, I've learned that it's important to visualize with as much detail as possible. Set an intention of what you wish to see and accomplish, and close your eyes. Engage all your senses. What do you see when you look around? Do you hear anything? Are there any distinct smells in the air? What are you wearing?

Then imagine the feeling of accomplishing everything you set out to do. If you can see it with your eyes closed, you can hold it with your eyes open. When you're done visualizing, you can solidify the experience by writing down everything you experienced and how it felt to accomplish your goals, understanding that it also takes massive action to make them happen.

TAKE ACTION

What follows is the visualization exercise I guide people through at my event. You can read through it, but I recommend recording yourself or someone else reading it aloud so you can close your eyes during the exercise, listening and focusing intentionally. If you would like me to walk you through this exercise personally, you can find my recording at *BestVersionEver.com*.

Take a deep breath in. Take in every life experience that has brought you to this moment. As you inhale, think of the capabilities your life and your mentors and your teachers have given you. Then, as you exhale, let go of everything you need to move past.

Imagine your future unfolding before you, like watching an actor on a movie screen. Allow images to come and go. Imagine you have a remote control in your hand to fast forward, rewind, or pause if you like. Right now, set an intention to see something happening that you've never seen before. It could be a moment or a new relationship.

I want you to see yourself overcoming adversity. I want you to see yourself harvesting the fruits of the contributions you're making in life. See image after image. You can sit with one or see yourself, again and again, emerging with new decisions and continually becoming the best version of yourself. What does it look like? How does it feel?

Now imagine yourself going back to your family or going back to your work. I want you to see yourself stepping into a new power, into a new strength, at your own pace, and in your own way. I want you to see yourself making new decisions, creating opportunities, demonstrating certainty, and letting go of doubt.

Imagine seeing yourself a year from now. Look around and see everything that's new and everything that's different. Imagine your work flourishing and your bank account growing. Now fast forward another year and another year, and realize that what is possible in a few years could be something you've never even thought of.

Imagine the most important people in your life as if they're standing right in front of you. Look in their eyes and see yourself creating greatness for others. Maybe it's your children; perhaps it's your husband or wife; maybe it's someone you've never met. See yourself bringing love, compassion, and generosity to others, and feel empathy coming from within that. Imagine being present with those people you're so lucky to have with you on this journey and seeing the amazing future you're creating for them.

As you see your life unfolding, I want you to imagine even further into the future: five, ten, fifteen years. Imagine looking at yourself in the mirror. I want you to see a stronger body with more energy, wisdom, and power than you've ever known. Imagine looking back at this moment, realizing that starting today, you made decision after decision to get here.

Now go twenty years into the future and see yourself able to do things you can't even do today, experiencing adventures for decades to come.

And now imagine a few decades later, when you realize that the number of remaining moments are not that many, and envision having lived the life you wanted to. Imagine the ripples you have left on others, the impact you've made on individuals, and the contribution you've made to society. I want you to see that you have touched so many lives.

Realize at this moment that you were born for a reason and are already living for that reason. You will contribute to this world beyond anything you've ever thought possible.

Now open your eyes.

* Adapted from Jon Berghoff's XCHANGE Approach, a method for designing questions and conversations that unlock potential in groups and individuals.

MASSIVE ACTION

In November 2015, I sat down to set my goals for the coming year. To get out of my comfort zone, I asked myself, *What would be so ridiculous that writing it down could put into motion the events to make it happen?* So I put pen to paper, and out came, "Meet Eddie Vedder." I even gave myself a deadline of October 1, 2016.

Every morning, I would repeat, "I will meet Eddie Vedder this year," and then take steps to make it happen. For instance, I knew of a charity organization that would connect you to almost anyone in exchange for a donation. When I reached out, they replied, "Probably not going to happen. He doesn't do those kinds of things." But that didn't deter me at all.

I found out he was playing a solo show about an hour from my house, so I asked the charity organization if this was maybe an opportunity. They asked me what my budget was, so I threw out $5,000. They countered with $40,000. Yes, you read that right. Forty. Thousand. Dollars.

I decided to play along and asked them for more details. About a month passed, and the reply appeared in my inbox. "Eddie will play a couple of songs at a charity luau dinner the night before the show. If you can increase your donation to $50,000, we can get you a meet and greet."

On a whim, I searched "Eddie Vedder Luau" and found the site for the charity event. $1,000 a plate for dinner. I bought a ticket and convinced my friend Justin to go with me.

All these thoughts about what I would say to Eddie went through my head. What questions would I ask? Would I get to thank him for providing the soundtrack to my entire life?

When we arrived at the charity event, I noticed on the check-in sheet that Eddie would be sitting at Table 18, along with actor Judd Apatow and pro surfer Kelly Slater. Five minutes later, I saw Eddie sitting at his table, surrounded by two bodyguards. After seeing three people turned away by the bodyguards, I thought, *Maybe this was a mistake.*

Suddenly the entire room stood up, including Eddie, and everyone applauded some guy who had given a speech. Then the two security guards headed toward an oncoming fan. I was behind them, so there were about ten feet between Eddie and me. This was my moment; it was now or never.

I walked up and tapped him on the back. He turned around and smiled as I said, "Hey man, I just wanted to say 'hi.'" A security guard came over and said something I didn't hear.

Eddie shook my hand and said, "Hi."

That's it—I met Eddie Vedder. I visualized it, and at the same time, it didn't go the way I expected. No photo. No conversation. Just a handshake. All before October 1st.

Sometimes people think that if they can imagine something happening, circumstances will magically align to make it happen for them. There is this idea that whatever you focus your thoughts, feelings, and beliefs on will come to you in a physical form. This is bullshit—you also have to take massive action. For instance, I met Eddie Vedder not solely by visualizing it but by imagining it happening *and* taking steps to make it happen. As Jim Carrey says, "You can't just visualize and then go eat a sandwich."

To live a life you've never lived before, you must see yourself becoming someone you have never been before—and then you must work to become that person. Goals can help you on this journey.

TAKE ACTION

Identify areas in your life where you've set goals in the past and didn't take action and achieve them. Were you relying on hope as a strategy, or was something else holding you back?

Let those negative thoughts go, and write down several actions you will take to help you achieve your goals.

GOAL SETTING

One year, I posted a video on social media about my upcoming goal-setting event. Not long after, my friend Adrian messaged me. He hadn't been able to make the event, but after seeing my video, he started thinking about what he wanted to achieve. He set a goal to obtain a motorcycle license, found out what that process entailed, and took the necessary actions to get it done—all within a week!

Most people don't have articulated goals. In fact, most New Year's resolutions fail because most people wait until New Year's Eve to set them. There's no deep thought put into the resolution, no real plan of action, and then they wake up late and hungover the next day with no motivation. Realizing they're off to a bad start, it's not uncommon for people to give up within the first week.

Hope is not a strategy. If you want to become your Best Version Ever, you have to make the time to brainstorm and narrow down your goals.

BRAINSTORMING

The ideas in your head are magic, so practice writing down anything that comes to mind. The power of brainstorming is that nothing is off-limits. Nothing is impossible at this moment.

However, don't list goals just because they sound good. Once I was in a room full of real estate agents setting goals. When one person set a goal to sell forty homes in the coming year, the next person said the same thing. Then the next person said an even higher amount. It's good to have someone to push you, but the goal has to be yours to maintain motivation. You have to know why you want it and why it is important to you; otherwise, the drive and passion won't be there.

AFTERTHOUGHTS

We often base our entire identities on things that have happened in the past and are no longer happening in this present moment. We limit ourselves by saying, "I'm not the kind of person who…" We divide our lives into days, weeks, and months and then say, "I'll start tomorrow," as if there is something more significant about tomorrow than right now.

But time is entirely relative (and often irrelevant). The present moment is all we have. So it's essential to realize that you can decide to start something new or even be someone new at any moment.

Don't ever say "I can't"—you just haven't done it yet. Instead, learn to reframe your mindset from "I can't" to "I haven't yet…"

To get started, there are six areas where you can brainstorm goals that you might pursue: Mind/Spirit, Health, Relationships, Adventure, Work, and Finance. I've included some examples below.

Mind/Spirit

These goals are related to your mental well-being and personal development. Examples include reading books, watching/listening to educational or motivational videos and podcasts, journaling, meditating, scheduling quiet time, reviewing goals frequently, starting a give-back fund and donating to charity, volunteering, signing up for an online course or seminar, and teaching others.

Health

These goals are related to your physical health and fitness. Examples include losing weight, exercising, eating healthy meals, tracking food, joining a gym, signing up for an obstacle race or marathon, watching less television, going to sleep earlier, waking up earlier, spending time outside, joining a sports league, and reducing caffeine/grains/sugar.

Relationships

These goals are related to your family, friends, and tribe. Examples include planning date nights and family dinners, socializing with family and friends, strengthening a relationship, reading a book on relationships, celebrating birthdays and anniversaries, identifying a friend you could hang with more, forgiving someone, and meeting new people.

Adventure

These goals are related to play and free time, things that make you feel alive. Examples include starting a new hobby, planning a vacation, going on a road trip, starting a bucket list, going skydiving, climbing a mountain, flying in a helicopter, learning a new language, learning to play a musical instrument, and moving somewhere new.

Work

These goals are related to what you do to generate income. Examples include structuring and time blocking your day, making to-do lists, clearing out email, doing what you love for work, studying and training to gain new skills, analyzing and improving on something a competitor is successful at, increasing sales and income, and optimizing marketing and social media.

Finance

These goals are related to managing money and investments. Examples include creating a budget and reviewing it often, going through bank statements regularly, creating a savings account and saving a percentage of income, creating a plan to pay off debt, starting a college fund, starting a retirement account, cutting expenses, building credit, and increasing net worth and investments.

GOALS

MIND/SPIRIT

_____

HEALTH

_____

RELATIONSHIPS

_____

ADVENTURE

_____

WORK

_____

FINANCE

_____

TAKE ACTION

Write down any goals that come to mind in each of the six areas we discussed. Think of things you've wanted to do, thought about doing, or started doing but never finished.

Some other questions you can consider while brainstorming:

- What aspects of your life and work are dying, and what new opportunities await you?
- Where do you see an opportunity opening up right now?
- See yourself or your community from above as if you were flying. What are you trying to achieve in this phase of your life?
- Imagine you're a young person looking at your current situation at the start of your journey. What advice would this young person give to you?
- Imagine that you are approaching the end of your life. Reflect on your entire life's journey. What would you want to see at that moment? What impact would you like your life to have on those closest to you? What advice might your future self give to your present self?
- Bring yourself back to the present and decide what you want to create. What is your vision for the next few years? Then describe any critical elements of your future that you wish to achieve in all aspects of your life.
- What sacrifices will you have to make to bring your vision to life? What old habits do you have to let go of?
- Where can you find help to realize your highest potential? Who can you count on to be your partners, teammates, and mentors? How can you align with and even elevate their vision, aspirations, and dreams?
- How might you go about taking action immediately?

Adapted from Jon Berghoff's XCHANGE Approach, a method for designing questions and conversations that unlock potential in groups and individuals.

NARROWING DOWN

My wife, some friends, and I went on a helicopter ride over the Great Blue Hole in Belize a few years back. I had already achieved many things I'd set out to do and wanted to try something different. I thought, *You know what? This is so much fun. I really want to get my helicopter pilot's license.*

As soon as I got home, I started researching what it takes to get licensed to fly a helicopter. I learned that it takes four years of school, which would take time away from work and life, but I thought, *All right. I could probably do that.* So I called a school and went out for an intro ride over San Diego.

Then I discovered that those four years of school would cost $60,000—and I'd still have to rent a helicopter to fly unless I spent another $200,000 to own one. It didn't take a lot of math to realize it would be cheaper to pay for someone else to fly me occasionally.

I realized, yes, getting my helicopter pilot's license may be attainable, and yes, I'd probably love it, but it was utterly irrelevant to me at that moment. It was not worthwhile because it would be a distraction from the things that were already working well in my life.

To determine which goals are worth pursuing, consider using the SMART goals framework, which we will now discuss in greater detail.

SMART Goals

Once you've written down your unfiltered dreams, you'll want to determine whether they are specific, measurable, attainable, relevant, and time-based. In other words, are they SMART?

Your goals should be:

- **Specific:** You can't just say, "I want to make more money," and expect it to happen. Instead, say, "I want to make $100,000 this year." Then you can identify who you need to become and what you need to do to attain that goal.
- **Measurable:** Don't say, "I want to lose weight." Instead, say, "I will lose one to two pounds weekly." Determine benchmarks to monitor your progress; that way, you can answer "Are you on track to reach your goal?" with a simple yes or no, with no ambiguity.
- **Attainable:** You can't expect to play drums for Pearl Jam if your skills aren't on par. You can't decide to become an air traffic controller at forty because that profession has an age limit. Your goal should be realistic based on your capabilities, which you have some control over, and external restrictions, which you don't.
- **Relevant:** Sometimes your dream is a distraction from what you could be doing or what you're best suited for. Decide whether your goal is worthwhile or whether now is the right time.
- **Time-Based:** Goals without timeframes will remain dreams; you are unlikely to take action if there are no time expectations. If you give yourself six months to reach your ideal weight, you'll take six months to reach your ideal weight; if you give yourself three months, you'll figure out what it takes to do it in three months. Be realistic about what you can do, but set a date that gives you a sense of urgency.

Look at your current list—if something isn't attainable or relevant, throw it out. From there, choose one or two main goals in each category that speak to you. Most people can't focus on more than that at a time, and you can always pursue other goals later as your Best Version Ever evolves.

But don't get hung up on making the "right" choice. One day, after my son Andrew had spent several years serving in the military, I asked him what his next career move was. He said, "I don't know. I don't want to make the wrong decision."

I told him there was no wrong decision. Every decision and experience brings you exactly where you need to be.

Seeing where my life is now, it may seem like I had made the "wrong" decision when I worked at a jail, but I didn't. Instead, I gained valuable experiences, made great friends, and learned to work on a team. In addition, talking to one thousand criminals daily gave me the skills to communicate well in everyday group settings, when I had previously been extremely introverted.

You never know how your next decision will affect your life, so start taking practical steps to pursue your goals now. No matter what you decide, it will be the "right" decision for where you are right now.

Practical Steps

Pay attention to the categories of your top goals. Look for imbalances. We all know someone who is crushing it in business but has a neglected relationship. Or someone who would rather party every weekend than spend time with their kids. Make sure your goals are helping you become a well-rounded human being.

Once you've identified and narrowed down your goals, make sure you're stretching yourself. Research shows that goals that are specific and challenging but still realistic lead to higher performance than generic goals like "Do my best." So if your initial goal is to sell ten houses per year, you could ask yourself what it would take to sell twenty.

Don't sell yourself short. Instead, expand your beliefs about what's possible. Real change happens just outside of your comfort zone, so don't limit the potential of your Best Version Ever by making your goals too easy.

Looking at your list, consider which are "finish line" goals and which are "continuous improvement" goals. For example, a finish line goal would be, "I will weigh 180 pounds by June 1st." A continuous improvement goal would be, "I will create the habits to maintain that weight."

SMART goals are typically finish-line goals, but remember that there is always a new challenge and opportunity for growth. Because of this, it may be helpful to think of the goals you want to achieve as "milestones" on the journey to becoming your Best Version Ever.

Get comfortable with the idea that you'll never cross a finish line on this journey; you are your most current Best Version Ever at every stage. You may achieve finish line goals along the way, but strive to evaluate and constantly evolve, not to reach an endpoint. Then find meaning in everything else that you do as well.

FINDING MEANING

Following the Great Fire of 1666, architect Christopher Wren was hired to rebuild St. Paul's Cathedral. His survey of the London skyline in 1671 brought him face-to-face with three workers laying bricks, one atop the other.

Christopher asked each of them what they were doing.

"I'm laying bricks," the first said.

"I'm building a wall," said the second.

When asked what he was doing, the third bricklayer replied with a smile, "I'm building a majestic cathedral for the glory of God."

Even when people do the same thing, they can choose to give it different meanings. We are each responsible for making our lives meaningful, and every moment is an opportunity to do so.

While you want to avoid doing something you hate, like some job your parents want you to do or that you took because it has benefits, our society sometimes overemphasizes "following your passion." Sorry, passion doesn't always pay the bills. You can be passionate about music and be a shitty singer or musician. You can be passionate about cooking and burn everything.

Recognize when your passions are priorities and when they're projects. When they're the latter, find the things you're interested in *and* really good at, and like the third bricklayer, find meaning in those priorities. Then ask yourself how you can use those skills and that work as a vehicle to bring about positive change in the world.

That's what I did with real estate. I might not love the trans-actional nature of the business, but I enjoy the human side of it: making connections, building trust, and helping people. In addition, I've used real estate sales as a vehicle to change the world around me by donating to worthy causes with each sale.

And when you find meaning in your continuous improvement, whether in the things you have to do or the goals you specifically set, you can celebrate "becoming" and "being" simultaneously.

TAKE ACTION

Write a letter to yourself. The letter will begin, "It is December 31st, and I am becoming my Best Version Ever because…"

Write the letter as if you have achieved every single goal you set out to achieve, and found meaning in the things you needed to do. The more detail, the better. What did you accomplish? How did it feel? Read it out loud several times, visualizing what it would feel like to have accom-plished everything you set out to do.

If you feel comfortable, read your letter out loud to friends and family. Then, when you speak your goals into the universe or hear someone share theirs, you can get clarity on your goals and how to become your Best Version Ever.

Finally, seal your letter in an envelope and write, "Open December 31st." Place the letter somewhere where you won't forget about it. Open it on December 31st and be amazed at what you accomplished that previ-ously seemed impossible.

IT IS DECEMBER 31
AND I AM BECOMING MY
BEST VERSION EVER:

MOVING FORWARD

You've probably never heard of John Kitchin, but ask anyone in Pacific Beach, California, who "SloMo" is, and they'll tell you. John spends all day rollerblading in slow motion down the boardwalk.

Is he homeless? Is he insane? What's his story?

He says, "Before SloMo, I became the typical, institutionalized, educated Western man. In other words, I was doing everything by the standards of society. And frankly, I intended to work myself into oblivion, and get old, and die. At this point, I'm just trying to get to the end of my life without becoming an asshole again."

John had a turning point, at which he gave up being a successful doctor to do what lights his fire: skating up and down the boardwalk in slow motion. People cheer him on, as he says, because he's "one person who got away, who escaped and got to real freedom." SloMo does what he loves, unapologetically.

Some people feel like the world happens to them, and others believe that they make the world happen. The life you desire is waiting for you, just on the other side of looking inward and making uncomfortable decisions.

We spend about a third of our lives sleeping and another third working, and we'll spend most of the remaining time disengaged. How will you react to the time you can't control, and how will you make the most of what you can? What do you want? What are you looking forward to? What goals will help get you there?

Consider: what does my Best Version Ever look like in three months? A year? Three years? Once you discover and begin pursuing your aim, you can create a daily, weekly, and monthly gameplan to execute it.

First, however, think of one thing you can do *right now* that will give you momentum toward your goals. Stop reading, close this book, and do it. Don't come back until you've taken action.

CHAPTER 3

GAMEPLAN

I went to bed thinking tomorrow would be the day I'd be productive. I didn't have anything on the calendar, so I'd wake up, enjoy some silence, have a cup of coffee, read, and exercise before I started working.

The alarm went off, and I reached over to silence it. Groggy and unable to see, I picked up my phone and opened a social media app. There were notifications from yesterday's post, and the early morning dopamine hit as the likes, reactions, and comments rolled in.

I refreshed my newsfeed, pulling down with my thumb and releasing it like the slot machine it mimics. I eagerly waited to see if I'd be rewarded with something exciting, if it would be nothing new, or if it would be what we more commonly see: an advertisement.

When it refreshed, I noticed a new social media notification, so I opened it and watched a hilarious video that my friend had sent.

I then went to the kitchen to make my first cup of coffee. While waiting for the brew, I wondered whether the Padres had won the previous night, but rather than check the score, I watched a seven-minute highlight video on the internet.

The video app knows me so well, and I couldn't resist watching the suggested videos that followed. I found myself going down various political rabbit holes, and when I saw a video that interested me, I copied the link to share it with a few close friends.

While using the messaging app to share the link, I noticed another friend had sent me his favorite podcast episode, which happened to be over two hours long. I started to listen.

A few minutes in, I thought, *What am I doing?*

I decided I would get back on track. So, remembering that Monday was trash day, I walked outside, unlocked the gate, and brought both of my trash cans to the street. Coming back to the house, I noticed the battery on the security camera was low, so I grabbed a replacement battery, switched it out, and put the drained battery on the charger.

Okay, where was I?

After checking social media, I forgot to put my phone on "Do Not Disturb," so it started ringing. A client called me, saying she was leaving town and asking if she needed to sign anything before leaving. Of course, I reassured her that she had signed everything, but I second-guessed myself and reviewed her file just in case.

It was now well after 9 a.m., I hadn't even started working, and I hadn't gotten to exercise.

We are bombarded by distractions daily, and often we react to these demands on our time instead of doing what we need or want to do. We have locks for our doors, alarms for our houses and cars, passwords for banking and computers…We protect everything we own, but we don't protect our time.

We all need a break from time to time, and you don't have to feel guilty about scrolling social media or watching fun videos when that's what you intend to do. However, when we act *unintentionally*, we can quickly become distracted by social media, trash day, or even our own thoughts. Giving in to these distractions can cause us to stray far from our goals.

Once you've established your aim, you'll want to create a gameplan so you are intentional about pursuing your Best Version Ever every day. You can do this through mapping and prioritization.

MAPPING

Now that you have determined the big goals you want to pursue, it's time to make time for them—by creating a gameplan for each one.

Your gameplan should map out all the milestones you'll need to reach to accomplish a goal, and all the tasks you'll need to complete to reach each milestone. Remember, what doesn't get scheduled doesn't get done, so it's essential to add milestones into your calendar, put concrete tasks into your schedule, and then protect that time.

Start with the end in mind. What do you want to accomplish this year and in the next few months? Things don't have to stop after a year, but it's challenging to plan further than a few months in life because internal (e.g., priorities) and external (e.g., market) factors constantly change. Even if your goal is a year out, it's best to plot out only a few months and then pivot if needed.

Working backward, consider: what do I need to do each month of the year to reach this goal? Next, determine the weekly tasks you must complete to achieve your monthly goals. Then, decide which tasks you must complete each day to achieve your weekly goals. Finally, think of one thing you can do right now to get started. This immediate action will give you momentum.

Ask yourself: who would I need to become, and what would I need to accomplish to reach this goal? What new actions would I need to start taking? What existing habits would I need to keep doing? What do I need to stop doing or do less of?

Now that you've mapped out the milestones and tasks that will move you closer to achieving your goals, it's time to start creating an ideal daily and weekly schedule for them.

TAKE ACTION

Consider the following questions:

- Who would I need to become to reach my goals?

Now for each goal, start creating your gameplan:

- What tasks can I complete monthly to reach my goal?
- What tasks can I complete weekly to reach my goal?
- What tasks can I complete daily to reach my goal?
- What can I do right now to give me momentum toward my goal?

Write down a few things that you will need to start doing, keep doing, and stop doing. These are the habits that will support or undermine your intentions.

GAME PLAN

MILESTONES

What goal do I
want to accomplish?

MONTHLY MILESTONES
What tasks can I complete
monthly to reach my goal?

WEEKLY MILESTONES
What tasks can I complete
weekly to reach my goal?

DAILY MILESTONES
What tasks can I complete
daily to reach my goal?

RIGHT NOW
What can I do right now to
give me momentum
toward my goal?

PLAN IT

New action I need
to **START** taking

Actions I need
to **KEEP** doing

Actions I need
to **STOP** doing

IDEAL SCHEDULE

It's easy to set goals—and map milestones and tasks—but we often forget that we have to discover what route we're going to take to reach them. We must check in with our goals along the way and ensure we're constantly progressing in the right direction.

Ideally, you want to dedicate a recurring time to plan your week in advance. For me, it's early Monday morning, but for many, it's Sunday, since that's often a day of rest and reflection. It doesn't matter what day it is, as long as you are consistent about taking time to review the week that has just passed and to set yourself up for success in the week to come. Guard this time by scheduling it into your calendar and setting reminders on your phone.

During your weekly review, ask yourself what time you are waking up and going to sleep. This defines the amount of time you'll be working with.

> ### AFTERTHOUGHTS
>
> Research shows that the blue light emitted from phones, tablets, and televisions signals your brain to suppress melatonin production. Melatonin is a sleep hormone that signals your brain to relax before bedtime. This reduction in melatonin can make it challenging to fall asleep, stay asleep, and feel alert the following day.
>
> Remember, your body and mind are like a battery; you need to allow them to recharge, so put the devices away. You might also consider buying the most comfortable mattress you can afford since you will spend about a third of your life sleeping. That way, you will wake up ready to go every day—and recover quickly when you burn the midnight oil.

Unless you're retired, you have to show up for work, so put that into your schedule. This may be the largest or second-largest time block in your schedule, along with sleep.

Put mealtimes into your schedule. You have to eat, and without a plan, you're more likely to eat junk food.

Next, plan your "you" time. These are the things that are essential to your well-being; without them, everything else suffers. Examples include exercise, hygiene, quiet time, and reading.

Schedule any time needed to care for and bond with family or significant others.

Now, what time do you have left to work on your goals? Start putting your daily and weekly tasks into your schedule. The most important things never slip through the cracks when you hold a place in your day for everything that matters to you.

IDEAL SCHEDULE

TIME	MON	TUES	WED	THURS	FRI	SAT	SUN
4:00 a.m.							
5:00 a.m.							
6:00 a.m.							
7:00 a.m.							
8:00 a.m.							
9:00 a.m.							
10:00 a.m.							
11:00 a.m.							
12:00 p.m.							
1:00 p.m.							
2:00 p.m.							
3:00 p.m.							
4:00 p.m.							
5:00 p.m.							
6:00 p.m.							
7:00 p.m.							
8:00 p.m.							
9:00 p.m.							
10:00 p.m.							

You may find it helpful to set a routine for the morning and evening. Routines involve conscious effort to maintain—getting to the gym does not happen on autopilot—but when you schedule them in, you don't have to think about what you're going to do every day.

For instance, I like to read, meditate, journal, and review my goals before I start my day, and I end my day reflecting on what went well and what could have gone better. Some people want to exercise when they wake up, others before they go to bed; some want to work for a few hours first thing in the morning, and others after coffee.

You may also consider identifying the factors that make you most productive. What time of day do you typically work best? When are you most motivated and energized? My best working hours are early in the morning. For one of my friends who produces records, it's the middle of the night.

Whatever the time, if you schedule your goals into your most productive hours, you can achieve them more effectively. If you instead fill those hours with distractions or chores, you'll be exhausted before you even have the chance to start working toward your Best Version Ever.

If you don't have time for your goals, look where you can cut back; for instance, the average person spends three to five hours daily on social media and checks their phone over one hundred times. You might want to wake up earlier, spend less time on mind-wasting distractions, or create lists to help you be more efficient.

We all have the same 168 hours each week—how will you spend yours?

TAKE ACTION

Once we've learned a new skill, our brains start doing it unconsciously, so we can easily forget significant growth and achievements. Tracking your progress can remind you to appreciate and celebrate your wins and help you discover what comes next.

Use the last hour of the day to reflect on the following questions:

- What did I do well today, and what could have gone better?
- What would make tomorrow extraordinary, and what do I need to prioritize to make it happen?

LISTS

Confession: I'm not naturally a planner. When I asked my wife about it, she laughed and said, "You totally wait until the last minute."

I've waited until the morning before a big trip to pack, inevitably forgotten a toothbrush or a belt, and had to buy it while I was gone. I've waited until the week before Christmas to buy gifts and then braved traffic to and from congested malls because any online orders I might have made wouldn't arrive on time.

One of the costliest mistakes I've ever made was when I forgot to negotiate a few days for my client to move out after selling her house. We had received an offer that allowed her the time to move out, so when that offer fell through and the next one came in, I thought a few days had already been written in the contract. This caused a panic when I realized days before closing that she would need to move out as soon as she signed all the paperwork.

I interrupted my relaxing Sunday to drive a moving truck to her house so my client could move in time. I felt so bad for the inconvenience that I even gave her a few thousand dollars in gifts to compensate for the trouble. That day, I decided that I would never complete another contract without first using a checklist. I was never again going to miss something that important.

Talking to my airline pilot friend, I learned that they also use checklists. It's easy to forget a crucial step when a procedure becomes automatic, and in a high-stakes job like flying, one misstep could cause a dire emergency. To avoid this, pilots use lists before start, after start, before takeoff, after takeoff, during their descent, during their approach, during their landing, etc.

To-do lists contain the tasks you want to complete on a specific day, and checklists contain a list of steps to follow through on those tasks. Over the years, I've become more proactive about using both.

Once I've created my ideal weekly and daily schedule, it's not enough for me to remember to do those things. If I don't have something in my face as a reminder at all times, I lose track of what I should be spending time on.

The best thing I've ever done to keep me on track is to have a daily habit tracker right next to me on my desk. I list the things I have to do daily to win each day and become my Best Version Ever. With the list right next to me, I am reminded of what needs to be done, especially when unexpected events throw my schedule off track.

Now that you've created your ideal schedule, create to-dos and checklists that will help you execute the tasks that are necessary for achieving your goals.

TO-DO LIST

- ☐ Meditation & Visualization
- ☐ Read - 1 Hour
- ☐ Journal
- ☐ Review Goals
- ☐ Exercise - 1 Hour
- ☐ Intermittent Fast
- ☐ Write Book
- ☐ Drums - 1 Hour
- ☐ Plan Tomorrow
- ☐
- ☐
- ☐
- ☐

- ☐
- ☐
- ☐
- ☐
- ☐
- ☐
- ☐
- ☐
- ☐
- ☐
- ☐
- ☐
- ☐

MAXIMIZING PRODUCTIVITY

It is rare for UPS trucks to turn left. Whenever possible, a carrier always makes right-hand turns.

This practice began in the 1970s, when route optimization software advised drivers to make right-hand turns to avoid turning through oncoming traffic at an intersection. Research by the US National Highway Traffic Safety Administration shows that left turns account for 60 percent of crashes when turning or crossing an intersection; only 3 percent involve right turns. In addition, even when there is a dedicated left-turn lane, turning left can add minutes to a commute. Despite carriers making many more turns, a test conducted by the television show *Mythbusters* found that right turns save fuel because trucks aren't left idling in traffic.

Today, an automated computer program determines the most efficient route for each UPS truck, almost exclusively involving right turns. This practice saves the company hundreds of millions of dollars in fuel, wages, and vehicle maintenance each year, and hundreds of millions of miles driven. Because of this, UPS has been able to expand its operations consistently.

UPS became a global force by implementing an efficient strategy to maximize its productivity. If you feel like there's not enough time each day or week to become *your* Best Version Ever, try a couple of these strategies to make the most of your time: time blocking, the minimum effective dose, and delegation.

TIME BLOCKING

We've already established that time is a limited commodity, and to optimize our time, we want to minimize distractions and maximize productivity. One strategy is to get into a "flow state" through time blocking.

Individuals in a flow state are wholly absorbed in whatever they are doing. Flow states of mind occur when we devote our full attention to something we are deeply committed to, intensely focused on, and fully immersed in. Then, suddenly, the mind stops talking, allowing us to focus without distraction. There is a sense that time has slowed down.

I get into a flow state by putting on a twenty-five-minute playlist. The music is instrumental because songs with lyrics make me want to sing along, but at the end of the playlist, a familiar rap song comes on to let me know my focus time is up. I stretch, walk around, grab a cup of coffee, and use the restroom. I avoid checking email or going on social media so that I don't fall down a rabbit hole. After a five-minute break, I start my playlist over again.

Research suggests that the average person is productive at work for no more than three hours per day, so blocking your time into periods of work and rest enables you to sustain productivity for longer stretches. For example, it can be forty minutes of work and ten minutes of rest or fifteen minutes of work and two minutes of rest—whatever your ratio, these intentional blocks of time can help you focus.

AFTERTHOUGHTS

Over the course of each day, the brain gets tired as the neurotransmitters essential for sustaining motivation, concentration, and productivity are drained. Because of this, it can be beneficial to reduce working times and increase the frequency of breaks as the day progresses. Additionally, if you move, exercise, or talk to people during your break, the brain will recharge faster than if you watch the news or scroll through social media.

THE MINIMUM EFFECTIVE DOSE

I know people who go to the gym all day, thinking that if one hour on the treadmill is good, surely two or three are better. They get stuck in a chronic cardio cycle, where they move so much that they see diminishing marginal returns for their efforts, which makes them think they need to move even more. They don't realize that too much intense exercise can damage your body, so you need to gauge the proper amount of exercise to build muscle.

In pharmacology, the minimum effective dose is the lowest dose that will yield the desired results, whereas anything more is a waste. For instance, water boils at 100 degrees Celsius; increasing the temperature won't cause it to be "more boiled." A higher temperature simply consumes more resources that could be used elsewhere.

Generally, this is the "work smarter, not harder" principle. You don't want to use more time and effort than you need to. Just because some is good doesn't mean more is better.

Vilfredo Pareto was an esteemed philosopher and economist who looked at various industries and discovered that, in general, 80 percent of our results come from 20 percent of our efforts. While it won't always be an exact 80/20 ratio, the point is that we can focus our efforts on the 20 percent that moves the needle instead of the 80 percent that produces marginal results.

I knew someone who applied this principle to his online presence. He had been blogging five times a week, but when he started blogging two or three days a week, he realized he still had the same number of subscribers. So cutting back didn't negatively affect his efficacy, and it gave him the freedom to pursue other things.

This isn't to say that you shouldn't give 100 percent—C's might get college degrees, but no one wants to see a surgeon who did the bare minimum to graduate. Instead, determine the 20 percent of activities that lead to the most success, prioritize them in your schedule, and then give them your full attention. You may even be able to delegate the other 80 percent.

That's how you get the greatest return on your time.

DELEGATION

Sometimes people put too much time into things they don't want to do and which they could delegate to someone else.

For instance, there's a real estate agent I've been working with forever who refuses to hire an assistant and believes it's easier to do all the administrative stuff (e.g., paperwork, emails) himself. He doesn't realize that spending a fraction of his income on delegating that work would free him up to sell more houses, pursue new interests, and continue becoming his Best Version Ever.

If you're creating or running a business and yard work takes a few hours of your time each week, consider the opportunity cost of not hiring someone else. Your earning potential could be far greater than what it costs to pay someone to do the yard work.

If you're trying to eat healthier, and the time it takes to prepare meals is your biggest hurdle, consider a meal prep service. Even though these services can cost more than buying and preparing food on your own, most people see significant time savings and less food waste, since they're not throwing away as much unused food.

The point is that delegating is worth considering when you have the money, when the tasks are not urgent or important, and when they can be done just as well—or better—by someone else. This strategy can help you regain more productive hours in your day instead of just effectively prioritizing the hours you have.

PRIORITIZATION

We've repeatedly established that we have a finite amount of time on earth, so don't let other people's priorities guide your life. Every time you say "yes" to something you don't want to do, you're saying "no" to the things that move you closer to your goals. If you don't guard your schedule, other people's priorities can unintentionally become your priorities.

At the same time, you want to be flexible enough to handle the things outside of your control. I like to build a buffer into my schedule by adding travel time before and after anything I have to drive to. I don't mind taking calls in the car during travel time, but I never want to schedule them so close together that I don't have time to prepare.

Adding a buffer can be invaluable when emergencies and obligations arise, such as when you and your kids get sick, your spouse gets locked out of the car, you get stuck in the rain, or you have to take your dogs to the groomers. If you don't have a buffer, or you have a negative mindset, you may think, *I didn't plan for that. It wasn't in my schedule. I feel like things are always happening to me.* But life doesn't happen to you; it just happens.

Remember, how you react—the meaning you place on what happens—determines your experience. So don't let unexpected things derail you from achieving your daily and weekly milestones.

If your schedule goes off track, recognize that you're human, pick yourself up, and regroup. Identify the most important things you still have to do, and reschedule your day around those priorities. If you handle your priorities, you've won the day, even if nothing else on your to-do list gets done.

For instance, I always try to exercise, read, practice drumming, and review my goals; these are the priorities that generally help me win my day. However, working on my book is a priority right now, and practicing drums has taken a backseat. Priorities can change, and that's okay.

LEARN TO SAY "NO"

To protect your schedule, there will be times when you have to say "no" to things that aren't a priority. You'll never be able to become your Best Version Ever if you give all your time to others, so consider keeping space open for your growth. You don't have to say "no" all the time, but practice saying "yes" a little less to make room for the life you're trying to live.

We sometimes have trouble saying "no" because it feels like we're rejecting someone, and we are afraid of disappointing them. So we take the path of least resistance and do things we don't want to do to keep everyone happy—everyone but us.

Saying "yes" to something always means saying "no" to something else. Remember why you're saying "no" and explain to the other person that you have a previous commitment. You can even schedule another time to meet up with them or indicate that you'll get back to them when you're available—that way, you keep the ball in your court without sidelining them entirely.

It's our responsibility to avoid acting like assholes, treat people with respect, and do our best not to criticize them. You can show someone you care about them, support their goals, and stay in touch, but you aren't responsible for anyone's happiness but your own. Happiness is a choice we all make, not one we let others make for us.

It is not your responsibility to please everyone around you. It is not your responsibility to control someone else's feelings or thoughts. Each person will respond however they see fit, and you simply have to leave space for them to do so.

Consider which hurts more: telling the truth and letting the other person move on, or facing the consequences of avoiding the truth? Most of the time, people will meet you where you are; if they don't, it may have been a one-sided relationship that's not worth pursuing.

BE WILLING TO SACRIFICE

Making room for your priorities sometimes means making sacrifices, like turning down things you want to do. As I was writing this book, for instance, I had to turn down several beach days and say "no" to playing drums more than I said "yes."

If you want to progress toward your most important goals, resist the instinct to give in to instant gratification. Long-term goals generally take priority over short-term pleasure.

But remember, while sacrifices help you maintain structure in your life, your priorities are not the be-all and end-all in your life. If you're flexible and maintain a positive mindset, you may discover that a seemingly derailed day leads to new opportunities. And if you're curious enough to say "yes" to those opportunities, they may change your life.

Who knows? You may be one conversation away from discovering your new life's purpose, or the most important relationship of your life may be waiting in the next room you enter. So prioritize what you can, but don't be so rigid that you never take a chance.

MOVING FORWARD

I have a colleague who had a bad reputation for being uncommunicative. He wouldn't respond to calls or emails, and once, I walked into his office to give him a document in person, and he insisted that I email it to him instead. Years after this incident, he texted me out of the blue, "Hey, we should go have coffee sometime."

Now, my instinct was, *No, we shouldn't.* Why would I want to do that, especially when I had other things to do? Having coffee with him was not in my schedule, not on any lists I had made, but this action was so out of character for him that something inside me said, *Go.*

I chose to remain curious. So I said, "Yes."

This was a defining moment in my life. I shuffled my scheduled tasks, prioritized what I could, and met him for coffee. There, we started talking about what it takes to build real estate teams, something I had not even considered at the time. He suggested I look into a particular coaching company, which I learned was hosting an event in Dallas.

At this event, there was a guy I'd never heard of talking on stage about the importance of having a morning routine. Hal Elrod's story about perseverance and making the most of every situation resonated with me.

I didn't see Hal for the remainder of the event, but when I got home, I chose to take action. I sent him a message on social media, "Hey man, saw you in Dallas, just noticed we live in the same city. If you ever want to hang out, let me know."

He wrote back, "Hey, what's your phone number?"

Long story short, Hal and I became friends. I went to Hal's event in San Diego, where I made other lifelong friendships and learned about the impact of giving back. I then built a real estate team, recruiting a bartender who became our top agent making seven figures a year, and a member at the local strength and conditioning gym, who now runs her own successful real estate brokerage. We started donating and have raised over $200,000 for various local charities. Now I'm writing this book.

All because I spontaneously said "yes" to a cup of coffee with an asshole.

The butterfly effect is the idea that the smallest action can cause ripples. So I challenge you to look back and see how many decisions led you to holding this book in your hands. To becoming your Best Version Ever.

What if you're creating a defining moment in your life today? What if, ten years from now, you can look back at today as a moment you chose to live a life full of purpose and meaning?

Your gameplan is important because it sets you up for the success you expect. Flexibility and curiosity, however, set you up for the success you don't expect, whether it's winning the day despite disruptions or changing the entire course of your life.

CHAPTER 4

IMMERSION

I tried to learn guitar when I was fifteen. Then I tried to learn guitar again when I was twenty-five. Then suddenly, I was thirty-eight, realizing, *Holy shit, had I actually stuck to guitar, I would be expert-level by now.*

All the times I had tried to learn guitar, I was self-taught. I never took steps to go beyond the basics, like finding a mentor or joining groups—I just learned enough chords to string together a few songs. I'd had motivation but not endurance. I didn't challenge myself when my skills plateaued, so I never got any better.

I decided it wasn't too late. I thought, *You know what? I'm determined to become an expert at a musical instrument, even if I'm fifty years old when that happens. I'm not going to quit this time.*

That's when I committed to drumming.

Using the anecdotal 10,000-hour rule, I estimated that if I could put in a thousand hours per year—two to three hours per day—I could become an expert-level drummer within ten years. So I took lessons, followed relevant online discussion forums, and watched instructional videos. I learned from expert drumming instructors at camps in Canada and Ireland, becoming exposed to various styles of music. I joined a school where they put you in a band with other adults who were learning instruments. I followed up on an ad from some guys looking for a drummer to jam with. I threw drumsticks in my bag whenever I traveled so that I could practice on hotel pillows.

All of these activities accelerated my progress, but hiring my own coach was the most beneficial thing I could've done. I'll never forget how during an in-person lesson, he said, "You know, you don't have to hit the drums as hard as you can for them to make a beautiful sound."

I'd had this idea that drummers have to hit every drum and every cymbal with as much muscle and energy as possible, but my coach was right. Through his observation, I noticed that the drums actually sounded better when I hit them half as hard and with more finesse. I would have never learned that through the one-way communication of watching internet videos.

Five years later, I've probably logged 5,000 hours playing drums. I've learned over two hundred songs. I've played with several bands. I've become fully immersed.

As you develop and implement your gameplan, you will simultaneously work on immersion through commitment, continual learning, and mentorship.

COMMITMENT

On the first day of class, Professor Jerry Uelsmann split his University of Florida photography students into two groups.

Those on the left side of the classroom would be in the "quantity" group. Their grade would depend only on the number of photos they produced, regardless of quality. Those on the right side of the classroom would be in the "quality" group. Their grade would be determined solely by the quality of one stellar image. They could only submit one photo, and it had to be their finest work—practically flawless.

At the end of the semester, he was shocked to discover that the quantity group submitted the highest-quality photographs. Those in the quality group had spent their time creating theories about what embodied the perfect photograph, but they submitted only one mediocre photo; those in the quantity group, in contrast, had spent their time immersing themselves in photography.

Without the pressure of producing one perfect photo, the quantity group had filled their days with taking photos, getting creative, trying various things, and learning from their mistakes. Their skills improved dramatically through the process of creating hundreds of photos. Their commitment to trying things out made the difference.

In the same way, if you watched a video of me playing now, you might think that drumming comes easily to me, but it doesn't. Those videos don't show my commitment: the late nights drumming by myself, all the times I said "no" to lunch with friends so I could practice, and the nine days I practiced for six to eight hours per day and getting blisters on my hands to prepare for a show.

In society, we reward winners and hide or ridicule failures, so only wins get celebrated publicly. We're reluctant to share "I messed up again today" or "Another failure in the books" online, so we often don't see the ten to twenty years of struggle and refinement it takes to become great at something. But when we only see the wins (and not the struggle), it's tempting to think there is an "easy button," a "secret," a "quick fix," which leads to the fallacy of overnight success.

Behind every "overnight success," there are years of focused effort, challenge, struggle, and rejection. For instance, a rock band will often seemingly "come out of nowhere" with a highly successful first album, only to release a follow-up that isn't nearly as popular. You don't see their ten years of struggle when they slept in vans and nailed down those great songs, but next thing you know, the record company wants them to replicate the success of their first album. The second time, they only have a year or two to produce an album, and they don't have nearly as much turmoil to draw from when writing.

Immersion requires you to put in the necessary time and effort, knowing that you will get value out of the struggle. If you see someone way better than you, chances are they just outwork you. They've committed. They've put in more hours. Those hours matter more than talent.

TAKE ACTION

Consider the following questions:

- What would you try if you knew you could not fail or knew that success was a certainty?
- What are you so committed to that you would give up a Friday night out with friends?
- What can you commit to for the next ten years?

CONTINUOUS LEARNING

On a day like any other, John Lee Dumas loaded up his iPod Nano with his favorite podcasts and headed out for a stroll. Having facilitated conversations as a public speaker in the US Army and in corporate finance, he loved podcasts that interviewed successful people, but he wished there was one that published an episode every day.

Then it hit him—he could become someone who interviewed the world's most successful entrepreneurs on a free, valuable, and daily podcast. Getting the chance to speak to thirty successful entrepreneurs every month, building relationships and possibly friendships, was a dream. He just needed to figure out how to make it happen.

John started thinking about the podcasts that inspired him. He noticed how the best hosts asked good questions, didn't talk too much, summarized key points, and released shorter episodes more frequently.

He decided he would conduct interviews that were no more

than twenty-five minutes but were packed with value. As a host, he would ensure his guests were prepared with stories and strategies from their past successes and failures, make sure that they were the focus of the episode, and summarize key lessons and takeaways for listeners. In addition, he would buy high-end audio equipment and release episodes frequently and consistently.

With his aim in place, John began immersing himself in what it takes to publish a podcast. He read three- and four-star reviews of other podcasts to identify shortcomings and opportunities. He researched the industry to determine the equipment to buy, how to set everything up, and how to attract great guests. He made a list of podcasts that inspired him and visited their websites, studied their business models, followed them on social media, and subscribed to their email newsletters. Then, understanding he couldn't get started alone, he found a mentor and joined an accountability group.

Over the next few months, with a lot of help from his mentor and accountability group, John built a multiplatform presence with a team of talented graphic designers, web developers, and other independent contractors. He connected with entrepreneurs at an event in NYC called Blog World, and he scheduled, recorded, and edited his first forty podcast episodes. Now John has published nearly 4,000 episodes of *Entrepreneurs on Fire*, generating over 2.5 million listens each month and over 125 million total downloads to date.

You may be thinking, *I don't have as much time or money to invest as John,* but even if you have time or financial barriers, you can always find ways to continuously learn and challenge yourself. Here are some immersion methods:

- **Internships:** If you dream of working in a particular field, you can volunteer your time and talents. It's a win-win for both parties: they get free help, and you get free training.
- **Written Content:** It's helpful to seek out people actively discussing the subject you are learning. You can buy or borrow books, subscribe to magazines, and browse internet articles and websites to get started.
- **Videos:** Watching videos on the internet and subscribing to your favorite instructors or performers can be helpful for learning tips and tricks, especially if a channel regularly releases new content.
- **Social Media:** It can be helpful to follow expert-level influencers in your chosen area who provide useful commentary and demonstrations for their followers.
- **Groups, Training, and Seminars:** Online and in-person groups, training, and seminars can allow you to network and learn from like-minded people.
- **Product Reviews:** It can be helpful to read product reviews when learning a new skill, even if you don't buy anything immediately. Reviews can help you understand the right tools for different projects, and you may also discover products that help you learn faster or perform better.

All of these learning methods have one thing in common: imitating others. In addition, they might even help you find a mentor, which is one of the best things you can do to become immersed.

IMITATION

Roger Bannister broke through the elusive four-minute-mile wall in 1954, running it in three minutes, fifty-nine seconds. For decades, runners had been trying unsuccessfully to reach that goal, but it turned out to be more of a mental challenge than a physical one: just forty-six days after Bannister ran his mile, an Australian runner broke his record. More than a thousand runners have run a mile in under four minutes since then. Once the world saw it was possible, people began to believe they could do it too.

From the day we're born, we begin imitating everyone around us: we learn our first words and gestures by listening to others. We pretend, play house, and play with toys based on what we see adults do. We mimic our friends' body language and interests, think that the clothes our favorite celebrities wear are "cool," and use others' opinions to create social structures in our heads.

Imitation is a fundamental part of achievement because studying others allows us to learn things effectively and quickly. When I built my real estate team, for instance, I looked at what other people were doing to see how I could imitate them. I even interviewed a top-performing agent, asking about her strategies and where she got her business. I saw her success and believed I could achieve success in real estate as well.

Most people who have achieved something at a high level of success in their field reach a point where they become sought out for their knowledge. They're invited to speak at conferences, are interviewed for podcasts, teach webinars, and often publish magazine and internet articles to share their experiences and knowledge. Therefore, it's essential to listen to their struggles and discover any lessons they've learned along the way. You may speed up the learning curve for yourself by avoiding some of the mistakes they've made, and at the same time, their experiences may prepare you for the struggles to come by just letting you know what to expect.

However, imitating others can only get you so far. Once you reach a certain level, you'll want to differentiate yourself.

DIFFERENTIATION

One way to differentiate yourself in a competitive environment is to do something no one else is doing. For instance, when Netflix started, it competed with Blockbuster; you could rent a movie by mail with Netflix or drive to Blockbuster to rent it. Eventually, Netflix did what no one else was doing: streaming video to your device, eliminating the hassle of physical products.

At my real estate company, we differentiated ourselves by donating a portion of each sale to charities. Involving all our stakeholders (e.g., clients, our agents, outside agents, and ancillary service providers), we started hosting huge events where we would raise over $10,000. No one was doing this at the time, and it inspired other companies to start giving back and make an impact within the community.

If you find that your progress toward your Best Version Ever plateaus, it may be because you're holding yourself back, so try something new. Of course, this requires effort, but originality arises when we continually strive to be more authentic and skilled than before. And who knows? You might write your own music, create your own business, or even change how your industry works.

As you reach new levels of success, you may even find that you're now the expert that others imitate. People may seek *you* out as a mentor, which may inspire you to innovate even more.

MENTORSHIP

Someone once gave me the business card of the president of a major mortgage company. I was still working as a corrections officer and had been thinking about learning how to write mortgage loans, so I immediately called him.

When we met, Tony was sixty-plus, with a rough voice from years of chain smoking that underscored his "old New York" style: straight-to-the-point smartass with a lighthearted side. While it was the responsibility of my parents and teachers to guide me growing up, Tony was the first person in my life to teach me things when he didn't have to. He saw something in me and decided to mentor me, asking nothing in return.

Once a week, I would use vacation time to drive two hours to sit at Tony's desk and learn about mortgage loans. He used the oldest calculator in the world to review loan applications, and through his example, I learned how to calculate income, debt ratios, and even payments by hand. Tony also taught me how to make friends with real estate agents, explaining how if I helped enough of them succeed, they would help me in return.

That's the value of having a mentor—having someone who can help you learn and keep you on track.

Watching videos or reading an article are forms of passive learning, like when a student receives information from a teacher and internalizes it without much reflection. Mentorship, in contrast, enables two-way communication; mentors can help you course-correct if they notice something's wrong, and you can ask questions if you don't know what to do. This turns on active learning.

In an academic setting, mentorship can take a formal or informal path, where a teacher facilitates intellectual development inside and outside the classroom. In a workplace, mentorship is usually conducted through formal or informal relationships to enable career advancement. In both cases, mentors help people improve their performance by sharing the setbacks they've encountered and suggesting corrections their mentee might make.

Research suggests that mentorship leads to better performance, career advancement, increased earnings, and greater job satisfaction. In addition, it improves recruitment, development, and retention. However, studies show that while about 75 percent of people believe mentors are necessary, only about one in three people work with one.

Let's remedy that by looking at how to find a mentor.

FINDING A MENTOR

Christine Comaford wrote a short, genuine letter to Steve Jobs, in which she declared her admiration for his accomplishments and offered to donate five hours of her time to his favorite nonprofit in exchange for five minutes of his time. She sent the letter via FedEx and called Steve Jobs's executive assistant to ensure it had arrived, building rapport over the phone.

Then Christine sent another letter. And another.

She called some more.

After seven FedEx letters and twelve phone calls, Steve's assistant said Steve wanted to talk. He agreed to meet in person and told her to "Bring a timer."

That five-minute meeting turned into a forty-five-minute meeting, which turned into a friendship.

Almost anyone can use Christine's straightforward approach to finding a mentor, but I suggest doing your research before reaching out to total strangers. If you can help them solve a problem or offer assistance, they may be more receptive to speaking with you.

Once you determine the skills you want help with, you can also find potential mentors in your community, including family, friends, and coworkers. If you don't already know a prospective mentor in your community, ask a mutual contact to make an introduction for you whenever possible.

In addition, you can find a group mentor instead of a one-on-one mentor. Sometimes called group coaching or a mastermind, the benefit of this method is that the group's collective wisdom is used to help each member.

Most prefer to let a relationship develop organically from conversations with a prospective mentor rather than asking straight-out about mentorship, and that's okay. Just remember to keep an open mind whenever you meet someone. If you stay curious and ask questions, you may find a mentor waiting in the next room you enter. They may even find you.

For instance, I've mentored many people in my life, but when I think of stories where neither of us knew we were looking for that kind of relationship, Garrett is the first to come to mind.

It was the World Cup, and even though we don't follow soccer, my friends and I thought watching the United States versus Ireland in an Irish bar at 8 a.m. sounded like a good idea. Later in the afternoon, we made our way to a few bars, and at the last one, I noticed a younger guy behind the bar working the entire crowd. I was too intoxicated to try and talk to him without sounding like an idiot, but I remember thinking, *He would be good at real estate.*

The bartender had been on my mind for two weeks when I happened to walk by the bar and decided to go in, in the middle of the day. On a Sunday. I sat at the bar, asked for water, and started talking to Garrett about real estate. He hadn't thought about it before, but it intrigued him enough that he signed up that day for classes to get his license.

I started training him, and without boring you, he's now the top agent in our company. Not only that, but we've become family. I was in his wedding, and we vacation and play sports together. We even played in a band together at my birthday party.

Be discerning when choosing (or being chosen by) a prospective mentor. Mentors can be cheerleaders, guides, and players in your life—but they have to *want* the responsibility of assisting you with transitions and challenging projects.

Often people choose to be mentors when they're older, when the best way to advance their personal growth is to support someone else. However, in some fields, someone with three to five years more experience than you might have better advice than someone decades ahead, since someone with more experience might not understand what you're currently going through.

In addition, your mentor will likely be someone who has already achieved something you've set out to do in the same field you're pursuing. For instance, someone in healthcare may not be the best mentor when starting in the restaurant industry.

When deciding whether to work with a prospective mentor, consider: is this person living the life you want, and have they ever been where you are now? Look at their mindset, health, and relationships; they could be a good fit if they have what you want. Also, look at their current and past situation; they need to understand what you're dealing with and your challenges. If they have been in your shoes, they can help you navigate the challenges you'll face.

Once you've found the right mentor, you will want to prepare yourself for working with them.

TAKE ACTION

Consider the following questions:

- Who can you send a FedEx to until they respond, and what cause can you contribute to that is dear to them?
- What questions can you prepare in advance of finding a mentor?
- Name three people who are living the life you want. How can you reach out to them as potential mentors, or how might they introduce you to a possible mentor?

BEING PREPARED

A mentor/mentee relationship is voluntary, so you will want to make the most of your time together.

Let your mentor know what you're learning, what you want help with, and why you're reaching out to them instead of someone else. Then make a plan so that they know what to expect. Your mentor will have time to consider how to support you if you send them a list of topics or questions before your meeting.

Be considerate of your mentor's time by taking care of the details, such as finding a meeting place or setting up a video call so they can just show up. However, be sure you don't overload your mentor with requests for their time, since they have personal lives and responsibilities.

Keep open lines of communication with your mentor. Tell them how you implement their suggestions, ask questions, and be prepared to take critiques. While criticism is meant to break you down, critiques are simply reviews you can learn from. Try listening with an open mind instead of formulating a defensive response while the other person is still talking. Before reacting, take a deep breath and assume positive intent.

Communication is two-way, so you may also offer your mentor feedback. Taking the time to acknowledge their efforts will demonstrate your appreciation for their contributions.

Giving feedback to your mentor can be as simple as asking yourself these questions:

- What have you learned and implemented from their guidance?
- How do you feel about their mentoring style?
- Could they be of more assistance in any areas?

Finally, send your mentor thank you notes and introduce them to others who can help them achieve *their* goals. These small gestures of gratitude can go a long way.

Together, you can both become your Best Versions Ever.

MOVING FORWARD

Legend has it that at a market in Paris, a woman approached Picasso and asked him to draw something on her napkin. He sat down, drew on the napkin, and handed it back—but not before asking for a million francs.

"How can you expect such a large amount of money?" she asked in shock. "That drawing only took you a few minutes!"

"No," he replied, "It took me forty years to learn to draw it in a few minutes."

Immersion requires a commitment to both learning and doing. As a society, we sometimes spend *too* much time studying and not enough time taking action. We read and read and watch and watch, but we don't *do*.

While learning is essential for becoming your Best Version Ever, I suggest reading no more than one or two books or watching more than a couple of videos before you start to try something new. Otherwise, you get stuck in analysis paralysis mode, refusing to move forward until you think you've got it down perfectly.

Perfect is the enemy of done. I know people who want to start a podcast, but they never will because they don't have the perfect office setup, the perfect microphone, the perfect website to host it on, or the perfect recordings. It's never going to be perfect; there will always be somewhere you can improve.

You must start the process and suck at something before getting close to good. It's been said that comparison is the thief of joy. Don't compare your initial skill to someone else's expertise because they were once where you are. Instead of letting someone else's skills discourage you from continuing, let it be motivation for you to practice longer and more consistently.

You will have okay moments and good moments, sprinkled with greatness in between. You just have to start.

CHAPTER 5

CONSISTENCY

When I was working as a corrections officer, I would eat in the cafeteria. The quality of the meals was only a few notches above jail food, *maybe* on par with fast food, but it was free.

Five years into that job, I was fifty pounds heavier. I hadn't noticed the extra weight as I was putting it on, and I didn't start seeing it until I looked at photos. I was living proof of how making poor food decisions consistently can make a massive difference in health—but I didn't do anything to change.

Then one day, I spoke to a guy who did marketing for musicians. He said, "Hey, do you want me to be brutally honest about what your band can do?" When I gave him my approval, he continued, "You could probably lose ten to twenty pounds. It's very noticeable in your face."

My initial reaction was to take his advice as criticism, but I shifted my mindset and instead took it as a critique I could grow from. I thought, *Wow. You know what? He's right.* That's when I made it a goal to become healthier.

However, eating well and working out consistently is hard work. For instance, I've signed up for gym memberships and then quit because of the time and expense, thinking I could do it on my own—and from time to time, my garage contains the remnants of failed attempts at creating a home gym.

I'm sure some of you have a similar situation in your house. A treadmill that collects laundry? A weight set that gathers dust?

The good news is that getting past initial resistance is the hardest part. Even Steven Spielberg, one of the most accomplished directors of all time, says that the most challenging thing about directing a film is getting out of the car. He, like all of us, constantly faces resistance.

The only thing I've found that moves the needle in all areas of my life is working out consistently: when I start my day with strenuous exercise, everything else is easier. The rest of my life is healthy when I'm healthy. So I make myself go.

I tell myself, *Just get in the car. Just drive there. Just get out of the car. Just walk inside.* It's routine—wash, rinse, repeat. I don't always like it, but it works.

Your gameplan involves scheduling and prioritizing your time, but to create sustainable lifestyle changes, you need to establish habits and use motivational techniques. By doing these things, I never reach more than ten pounds over my ideal weight—and that's when I've been eating tacos in Mexico for five days. Even then, I know how to return to my healthy lifestyle because I've learned consistency.

HABITS

Habits usually occur in response to a specific trigger, with little to no conscious thought. For example, waking up can trigger you to check your phone, getting in your car can trigger you to fasten your seatbelt and look for music or a podcast, and attending a work meeting can trigger you to pour a cup of coffee. No matter how much we wish our lives were different each day, repeating the same daily habits is not uncommon—and it allows us to free our minds for other decisions.

Unlike habits with little thought, routines like cleaning your house, making your bed, and getting dressed require focused thought. Before something can become a habit, it has to start as a routine. For instance, as kids, our parents told us to put our seatbelts on, but we would forget. They would say to us again. And again. We got into the routine, and before we knew it, it was a habit.

From the time we wake up, we make decisions: *When should I leave for work? When should I have lunch? Should I speak at the team meeting? Should I go to the gym?* Making these decisions expends mental energy, and the more energy we expend, the less we have for making other decisions.

Imagine you're shopping online and comparing ten versions of the same product. You've spent hours reading hundreds of reviews, but every product has several one- or two-star reviews, which makes you think you could be making a mistake despite the product's high average rating. This is decision fatigue, and it's why Amazon has Amazon's Choice—so you don't have to decide yourself.

You face the same situation in your daily life. After working eight hours, you get home and realize you have a few healthy ingredients in the fridge, but you would have to choose how to prepare your entrée, which side dish to make, and what ingredients to use, so you opt for fast food delivery instead. After a long day of decision-making, you are fatigued, which leads to poor decisions.

Decision fatigue makes it difficult to resist the urge to do what's easy and impairs your ability to work consistently toward your Best Version Ever. The most effective way to combat this is to create routines that align with your goals; once those routines become sustainable habits, they no longer affect your decision-making capabilities.

For instance, Steve Jobs had a trademark look: black turtleneck, blue jeans, and New Balance shoes. Why? He didn't have to decide about his outfit every day, which cleared his mind up for other decisions.

So if you want to go to the gym, try sleeping in gym clothes with your shoes next to your bed. Then you'll wake up ready to go instead of wondering *if* you will go. If you want to wake up earlier, set your alarm and put your phone across the room. You'll have to physically move to turn it off, waking you up *before* you decide to go back to sleep. Eventually those new habits will replace the old ones, creating the life you want without the overwhelm that decision fatigue causes.

ESTABLISHING HABITS

When I decided to make flossing a habit, I kept a piece of paper that said "Floss" next to my computer. Every day, I would see that reminder and would bring a flosser into the shower. Then, after flossing my teeth, I would make a basketball shot from the shower, landing the flosser in the sink. When I got out, I would throw the flosser away and check off that task for the day.

Now I don't even think about it anymore—I grab a flosser before I get into the shower. (And I haven't had a cavity in years.)

Establishing habits can be difficult, so here are some strategies to get you started:

- **Make things obvious. Make them foolproof:** Ask yourself, *How do I set up my environment so that it would be impossible for me NOT to complete this task?* For instance, if you want to drink more water, put your water bottle on your desk or your nightstand.
- **Anchoring:** Pair a new habit you're trying to solidify with an existing routine. For instance, if you drink coffee every day and aim to meditate every morning, you can meditate for ten minutes while your coffee is brewing.
- **Multitask:** Combine something you have to do with something you want to do. For instance, I want to spend fifteen to twenty minutes a day working on hand and foot speed exercises to improve my drumming; the task is not very exciting, but I listen to an audiobook or podcast during that time.
- **Minimize distractions:** Remove the things that impair your ability to focus from your environment; for instance, turn off social media notifications for specific periods of time. This goes back to controlling your schedule—if you let your phone notifications constantly interrupt your day, you lose valuable time.

It's important to keep your aim in mind. At some point, the things that used to be challenging to you will become boring, so continue to visualize the person you're becoming as a way to maintain momentum. Keep establishing habits and tracking your progress so that you can make consistent, incremental improvements.

TRACKING PROGRESS

Early in our marriage, my wife and I would argue regularly, and it was almost always about how we were co-parenting. The kids were entering their teenage years, and while I was used to doing things the way I always had, my wife had a different perspective working in education and youth development.

One day, we joked that we should keep a sign around the house, like those on construction job sites that say, "14 days since the last safety incident." After a few minutes, we thought, *Wait. What if we DID do that?*

We put a whiteboard on an easel, moving it around from time to time so that it was in our faces, and the results were pretty amazing. We made it to 100 days without an incident before we celebrated and decided we could stop tracking it. We had formed a habit of really thinking before reacting, and the constant visual reminder was a crucial piece.

There's something about seeing a streak of success and not wanting to break it. My wife and I both admitted that several times we wanted to argue our point and blow things up, but knowing that we had a consecutive streak of days without an incident kept us in check. Seeing the sign daily reminded us that there were other ways to communicate besides fighting. It forced us to hear where the other person was coming from and consider their perspective.

Often people don't even realize they're overfighting, overspending, or overeating when it's a habit—in general, we underestimate the frequency with which we do certain things. For instance, a study at Cornell University found that healthy people underestimate calorie intake by about 20 percent, while overweight people underestimate it by about 40 percent. When we check in with ourselves, however, we don't have to rely on our gut feelings and opinions; tracking provides us with facts we can use as a baseline for comparison.

Studies show that people are more likely to achieve their goals if they monitor their progress. The more frequently we monitor our goals, the greater the likelihood of our success; the chances of success are even higher if we log our progress or publicly share it.

For instance, my wife and her friends do these ring challenges on their smartwatches. There are three rings corresponding to how much they've moved, how much they've exercised, and how much time they've spent standing. They do challenges where they put money in a pot and must close all their rings daily to stay in the challenge. Tracking has caused them to pay attention to how active they are, and it's not uncommon for them to exercise late at night or even run in place at the last minute to close the rings.

Using a tracking system can help you hold yourself accountable, but it can also help you see the progress you've made. Too often, we lose motivation because we don't feel like we're achieving anything, but seeing and celebrating incremental gains can inspire you to keep going. Awareness of where you are, where you want to be, and what will help you get there motivates you to become your Best Version Ever.

TAKE ACTION

Use a weekly chart of to-dos (like the following example) to track how often you spend time doing specific things.

DAILY HABIT TRACKER

NEW HABIT	MON	TUES	WED	THURS	FRI	SAT	SUN	ACHIEVED	GOAL
Read 30 Minutes	X	X		X	X	X		5	5
Floss	X	X	X	X	X	X	X	7	7
Excercise	X		X		X	X		4	4

MOTIVATIONAL TECHNIQUES

In 2016, I blindly joined a small accountability group. Our group of five met every two weeks to discuss what was going well, how we were progressing on reaching our goals, and what we could use help with. Each meeting ended with us declaring what we would like to be held accountable for in the coming weeks.

In most cases, the consequence of not meeting your accountability goals resulted in a discussion about where someone went off track, what they could have done differently, and what they could change in the future. But less than a year after joining the group, I heard, "Mario, it's time to eat your puppy chow."

Two weeks before, Mario had texted us, "I have a few gyms in mind and will pull the trigger and complete my first workout before the end of the week, or I'll eat dog food." Now at our meeting, he was having a friendly debate with Mark about the text. Mario had technically worked out, but not at a new gym as his message implied, and Mark was holding him to the fire.

Mark replied, "A sin has been committed against this group, and now someone needs to eat dog food. If you don't eat it, I will."

Two weeks later, Mario ate the puppy chow.

Those guys have since become some of my best friends. Not a month has passed without us meeting at least twice to talk about life, goals, and building each other up. We've seen each other at our best and worst moments and been there for each other through it all.

This extreme accountability is only one of many techniques you can use to motivate yourself as you become your Best Version Ever. Whether creating an inspiring workspace or avoiding the threat of pain, the important thing is that you find the motivational techniques that work for you.

PEOPLE, PLEASURE, PAIN

When I was a kid, I read one of the oldest tricks in the book to get rid of a bad habit. The author said to place a rubber band around your wrist and snap it whenever you get off track. While you shouldn't injure yourself, the sting of the band should be hard enough that your brain would associate the negative feeling with the bad habit. You should then tell yourself to stop thinking about the habit you're trying to avoid and even replace it with a positive thought, like how much better you'll feel when you don't have this bad habit anymore. After a while, you would most likely give up the bad habit to avoid the rubber band's sting.

This is an example of using pain to motivate yourself, but there are three categories of motivators you can use to help you maintain the habits that bring you closer to achieving your Best Version Ever: people, pleasure, *and* pain.

First, let's talk about **people**. There's no turning back when you share your intentions with people because you don't want to disappoint friends and loved ones:

- **Accountability partners:** Find an accountability partner or start an accountability group with which you can check in regularly. Because we're social creatures, we enjoy praise and recognition for our work, but don't choose someone who will only give you positive feedback. Your friends or spouse may go easy on you, so you want to find a partner who will hold you to your commitments—someone who will refuse to cosign your bullshit.

- **Accountability groups:** Having multiple people hold you accountable for your daily and weekly progress is an excellent way to stay on top of whatever you're working toward, so start or join an accountability group. These groups allow you to see how other people implement strategies to accomplish their goals, and they're also a perfect opportunity to make new friends.

- **Public commitments:** To stay motivated, you can tell everyone you know who you're becoming. Post a video about your goals on social media, tagging friends and even competition. Share regular updates on your progress. Public commitments often inspire people to follow through.

- **Helping others:** Sometimes people are motivated by helping others. For instance, philanthropists are willing to trade money to help create a better world; they want to make a difference in people's lives to create a brighter future.

Second, **pleasure**. In moderation, pleasure can be just as effective as people for staying motivated:

- **External rewards:** If you use external rewards, you might tell yourself, "Once I do X, I will treat myself with Y." That could be a cheat meal, a purchase, or an experience—just don't reward yourself so often that you undermine your goals, like eating chocolate cake every evening after completing your workout.

- **Internal rewards:** Often people tend to pursue inner rewards and withdraw from external ones as they age; the feeling they get from seeing their progress and achievements *becomes* the reward. For instance, if you are active and eat well, you will start to feel healthier, allowing you to spend more time with loved ones. This can evoke the same, or greater, feelings of pleasure as a physical object.

Third, **pain.** If you're having trouble staying motivated, the threat of pain can keep you on track:

- **Money:** Sign up for an expensive gym membership. Write a check to a cause that doesn't align with your core values and tell an accountability partner to send it if you don't follow through on your intentions. No one wants to waste money, so the threat of losing it unnecessarily can be motivational.
- **Diet:** Understanding the pains that come from being in poor health can be a motivator in itself. Our eating habits form who we are physically, so the threat of aches and diseases can motivate changes in diet.
- **Exercise:** Similarly, the threat of aches and diseases can motivate you to begin or continue exercising. You can also use the pain of exercise to inspire you to complete other goals. For instance, in boot camp, it's common to have to do push-ups or sit-ups as a consequence of not performing a task. You may even find that the "pain" becomes "pleasure" as you get stronger and healthier.

Whichever strategies you try, be sure you're clear on exactly what you're motivating yourself with and why. You may find that what works is different from what you initially imagined.

TAKE ACTION

Set up a time and frequency to check in with an accountability partner. Ask your accountability partner for feedback on your progress. Ask them to withhold a reward until you've shown consistent habits or until you've met a key milestone.

Ask your accountability partner to hold on to a check written out to your biggest competitor or the political party you're not affiliated with. (This has to be a scary amount of money, not just $10.) Tell them to send the check if you don't meet your goals.

Ask people to comment on your social media videos/posts so that they get notified whenever you share an update.

CREATING YOUR ENVIRONMENT

I love milk chocolate-covered almonds so much that I will annihilate an entire bag in one sitting—but eating handfuls of candy at a time interferes with my aim to be the healthiest version of myself, so I refuse to buy them. Once I even begged my wife to stop buying them because if they were in the pantry, I couldn't control myself.

Whether you like it or not, our environment plays a prominent role in influencing our decisions. It can be a source of support or distraction, so to establish and maintain habits that align with our Best Version Ever, we want to create an environment that motivates us to succeed. We have to create the places and include the people that enable us to be productive and respond to situations as our best selves.

THE PLACES

The first strategy to create your environment is separating where you sleep from where you work. The Division of Sleep Medicine at Harvard Medical School recommends "keeping computers, TVs, and work materials out of the room will strengthen the mental association between your bedroom and sleep." In other words, this separation will allow you to get better sleep *and* do better work. After all, it's hard to feel motivated to work if your body and mind think it's time to sleep.

You can also adjust your environment based on your senses. One study found that students tested better in a temperature-controlled room than in an environment with extremely hot temperatures; others showed that dim lighting could reduce productivity and fluorescent lighting could cause headaches; others found that classical music improved concentration. While what works varies from person to person, it can be helpful to learn the temperature, lighting, and sounds that support or distract you.

Next, you can identify other distractions in your environment. For instance, delete any apps on your phone preventing you from achieving your goals; throw out any foods in your fridge that you know you shouldn't eat. The more distractions you remove from your life, the less willpower you'll need, because you can't give in to a temptation that is no longer there.

Once you've removed distractions from your environment, you can add things that inspire you. For instance, my office includes Pearl Jam posters, plants, and a sign that says, "Three words of inspiration: You're gonna die." Some may think that's morbid, but it reminds me that I won't be here in a hundred years. It makes me think, *Do I really want to scroll right now? Is that the best use of my time?*

However, even when we've set up our environment to motivate our success, we all need to take a break and go somewhere different once in a while. One study showed that participants who spent fifty minutes walking through a forest experienced less anxiety, less negativity, more positive emotions, and greater performance on memory tasks than those who walked along a four-lane city road. Nature is one of the greatest motivators in life.

Sometimes all it takes to regain motivation is getting in your car and driving to a new coffee shop, the library, or a park. I'm fortunate to live near the beach and often journal or think to myself while staring at the waves. The point is that altering your perspective by changing the space you're in can prompt your brain to think differently, just as the people in your environment affect how you perceive yourself.

THE PEOPLE

A violinist stood inside a subway station and began playing. During his forty-three-minute performance, he played six pieces by Bach, music so majestic that it has stood the test of time. Thousands of commuters passed through the station, many on their way to work.

A few minutes had passed before someone noticed the musician playing. One minute later, a woman gave a dollar tip without stopping. A few more passersby paused for brief moments to listen, then continued on their way.

Even though twenty-seven people donated money to the musician, most continued with their business; only seven watched him play. When the musician finished his set, he quietly packed up his things. No one applauded or even noticed.

Nobody knew that the violinist was Joshua Bell, one of the world's greatest musicians.

Three days before performing in the subway, Joshua sold out Boston's grand Symphony Hall, where seats average $100 apiece. In the subway, he played some of the most elegant music ever created on a violin worth $3.5 million and earned only $32 in donations.

This experiment begs several questions:

- Are we able to recognize talent in unexpected circumstances?
- If no one noticed one of the best musicians in the world playing in a subway, what else do we pass by without noticing?
- How do others' perceptions of us affect the way we perceive ourselves?

As humans, we tend to form strong social connections with those who share our defining characteristics (e.g., age, gender, ethnicity, socioeconomic status, personal beliefs); we then modify our behaviors, choices, and attitudes to make ourselves seem more relatable to them. This is called homophily.

As we spend time with the people in our environment, their habits and thoughts greatly influence us. Had Joshua not known better, or had he been someone else, the disengagement of people in the subway might have made him believe that his talent was not worthy of the Symphony Hall. As a result, he might have limited his own potential.

Understanding that the people in your environment either support or hinder your potential can help us recognize why some people are held back by their circumstances while others overcome them: it's all about what you believe is possible. That's why it is so important, whenever possible, to surround yourself with people who believe in you and will motivate you to become your Best Version Ever.

MOVING FORWARD

In *The Karate Kid*, Daniel is bullied at school because he's the new kid in town. After getting his ass kicked a few times, he decides to read a book about karate, but he doesn't see any development in his skills until the repairman at his apartment, Mr. Miyagi, offers to teach him.

On Daniel's first day, he is given a sponge and taught how to wash and wax Mr. Miyagi's cars. On the second day, he sands a deck. On the third, he paints his teacher's fence. On the fourth, he paints his house. At this point, Daniel feels confused and complains that Mr. Miyagi is asking him to do chores instead of teaching him karate.

Then Mr. Miyagi shows Daniel that he can block punches and kicks using the motions of waxing a car, sanding a deck, and painting the fence and house. Mr. Miyagi used the chores to teach Daniel the motions needed for self-defense, and Daniel's muscle memory was developed through the repetitive nature of the labor.

Just like Daniel, we can't learn most things merely from reading a book or watching a video; we must learn the motions by *doing*. As you become your Best Version Ever, you'll find that the MAGIC formula builds on itself; the more consistently you practice the recommended techniques, the more instinctual they'll feel.

CHAPTER 6

BECOMING

Before I had the coffee that changed my life, I was resting. My business was successful, and I was enjoying the fact that I was not working hard, not striving.

After that coffee, I was inspired to build my real estate team. I took the risk of reaching out to people I thought could make good real estate agents, and I hoped they would take the risk of working with me. I was vulnerable and authentic in starting my goal planning event, and my attendees reciprocated. I identified ways to give back to my community and grew much in return.

Three years later, my team was running on autopilot, I sold my business, and I took up drumming as my new project. I was in another restful season—until I got bored.

Now I am leading several real estate teams, coaching goal achievers nationwide, expanding my event, and writing a book. I expect things will settle in a few years, and I'll rest again, and that's okay. I'm trying to maintain balance because I want to live as long as possible.

Some of my friends don't recognize that life is fun, and that we can always find a reason to wake up and experience something. They ask, "Why do you want to live to be a hundred years old? You want to be lying in bed wearing diapers?"

I reply, "No. You'll be shitting yourself while I still walk three miles a day."

Our lives have whatever meaning we give them, and at the end of the day, it's essential to realize that our success isn't dependent on being effective cogs in the economic machine. Ultimately we're here to love, play, and become who we are.

Too many people think they must wake up early and be part of the "5 a.m. Club" to succeed. Then that doesn't seem good enough, so they join the "4:30 a.m. Club," and then when that isn't good enough, they join the "4 a.m. Club"—and so it goes until they grind themselves to a slow death. Look, I'm all for periods where you're on a mission, and if 4 a.m. is the only time you can carve out to do the work of becoming, then that's great. But it's not sustainable.

Life is like an ocean wave: you have periods where the tides of progress are building, but once they peak, there's a crash. Work is not meant to be sustained forever. Like the tides receding, you want to rest, recover, and enjoy the fruits of your labor until you're ready to slowly build up again.

Most of us overwork and under-sleep ourselves in the first half of our lives, trading our health and relationships for money, and then we spend money in the second half of our lives trying to get our health and relationships back. Part of becoming is allowing yourself to rest so that you can refocus, pursue connection, and give back.

REFOCUSING

It's hard to remember when Starbucks wasn't on every street corner, mall, and airport, but in 2008, the coffee franchise suffered a massive loss of customers.

At the time, Starbucks expanded into many areas, producing CDs, publishing books, and selling DVDs. Kiosks filled the once cozy and atmospheric stores. New espresso machines installed in stores to increase efficiency were too tall and blocked employees from engaging with customers. Bagged coffee grounds lacked the pervasive aroma of freshly ground coffee. All of this together "created the dilution of the experience," which led to Starbucks' stock price dropping by fifty percent.

Starbucks founder Howard Schultz said during the crisis, "We desperately need to...get back to the core and make the changes necessary to evoke the heritage, the tradition, and the passion that we all have for the true Starbucks Experience." Over the course of a year, he closed nearly one thousand underperforming stores, halted all operations for one day to retrain staff, and invited all store managers to New Orleans. There, Starbucks partners volunteered ~50,000 hours to restore the damage of Hurricane Katrina while reconnecting with the company's overall vision and purpose.

After the refocus, Starbucks doubled in market share and earnings. "If we hadn't had New Orleans," Schultz said, "we wouldn't have turned things around."

Everyone faces setbacks or experiences burnout at times, even massive corporations like Starbucks. As unsettling as those times can be, they're an expected part of becoming your Best Version Ever.

Sometimes all you need to recharge is to rest, but if you find you need to refocus, there are a few things you can do:

- **Reframe your Mindset:** See setbacks as learning opportunities. Where did you fail? What caused you to get off track, and how do you avoid that in the future? How could choosing to become your Best Version Ever right now be a significant and fulfilling experience for you?
- **Reconnect with your Aim:** Why did you initially decide to begin the journey toward becoming your Best Version Ever? In what ways does becoming your Best Version Ever benefit family, friends, and the world around you? What goals will help you on your journey?
- **Go back to your Gameplan:** Starting with a specific goal, work backward to see where you got off track. What do you need to do daily, weekly, and monthly to continue the journey?
- **Seek Immersion wherever possible:** Research people and things that inspire you, and try new immersion tactics. Reaffirm your commitment to learning and growing, and reach out to an accountability partner or mentor you've lost touch with.
- **Know that Consistency is a choice:** Recognize that even if you can't win the day, you can win the moment: you can decide to start over at any time and make that choice consistently. Remember, even consistent, incremental improvements result in huge gains over time.

Running a marathon starts with one step, one foot in front of the other. It's painful and doesn't seem like you're going anywhere, but you cross the finish line four hours later. It's the same principle with your Best Version Ever: restart one step at a time. If you've fallen off your fitness goals, start by taking a one-minute walk; then add a minute every day. If you've been eating like shit, eat one healthy meal today; then eat two tomorrow.

Take a small step again and again, and you'll soon find yourself connecting with people and your goals.

CONNECTION

Years ago, I reconnected with an old friend on social media. She had a crush on me in junior high, but I thought she was a nerd. Then we went to different high schools, and I didn't see her again until our senior year, when we worked at the same pizza restaurant. I thought she was cool, and we had a mutual attraction at the time, but I was preparing to be a teenage father, so we soon went our separate ways.

More than ten years later, we were both single again, and I decided to reach out. I would message her a few times here and there, but we would only have surface-level conversations. For example, I would say, "Hey, we should grab a beer sometime," and she'd say, "Yeah, we should," but we would never pick a date. Or I'd invite her to a party at my house, but something would "come up," and she never made it.

One night in April I thought, *I'm going to call her on the phone right now. What's the worst that can happen? She won't answer. Who cares? I haven't talked to her in ten years anyway.*

I called, and she answered. She was so shocked that I was calling her, and I was so shocked that I had actually called her, that we talked for two hours.

That call changed our dynamic. I was always the one reaching out, but in August, she reached out to me, asking if I wanted to get together. I remember thinking, *Yeah, right. She's just going to cancel like she always does.* But I said, "Sure, let's do it," and we set a date in September.

When the date was approaching, she said, "I can't do Friday, but I could do Saturday." I thought, *Here we go. Here's the cancellation coming.* I changed plans with her, but I was sure she wouldn't show up.

But she showed up, we went out, I proposed by the end of the year, and now we've been married for ten.

Humans are social creatures; we're wired to be with other people. Our survival has always depended on belonging to a group. Studies show that our close relationships are the best predictor of long and happy lives—more than class, intelligence, or genes. Our relationships directly affect our health, so no matter what season of life you're in, it's vital to prioritize relationships with others.

Because building and maintaining relationships takes work, you'll want to treat your relationships the same way you would any other goal. When you get caught up in the business of life, of living your Best Version Ever, the effort and planning you put into your relationships will determine how close they are.

Don't be vague. Think about what you want your relationship to look like and how often you wish to reach out. Then, directly ask, "Hey, want to grab lunch?" If you get a "yes," put something on the calendar immediately. We tend to say "yes" and then never plan anything, and things get forgotten.

Sometimes connection may feel one-way, and sometimes that's okay. It's not all or nothing. You don't need someone else's participation to love them or to be the best friend you can be. Sometimes people are at different stages in their lives, and you just have to meet them where they are. For instance, if they only want to talk on the phone but don't want to get together, make that work. If they only reply to your text messages but don't answer the phone, work with that.

However, if connecting feels like pulling teeth, it may be worth considering whether it's a relationship you want to maintain. Sometimes a relationship isn't as important to the other person, and it may benefit you to direct your energy toward being vulnerable with those who want connection.

VULNERABILITY

Whether presenting something we've worked on or expressing our feelings, we are often afraid to put ourselves out there. For instance, I shared a few pages of this book with close friends before it was published, which made me uncomfortable. I started to feel imposter syndrome, wondering, *Who am I to write a book?*

We were raised in a world where vulnerability is typically associated with failure, and connecting with our feelings is seen as weakness. We don't realize that when we expose our ideas, thoughts, and opinions to external critique, we're presented with an opportunity to learn something new or build deeper relationships. Vulnerability does not require us to share all of our personal details, but the ability to recognize when to share and when to remain silent is a sign of healthy vulnerability.

Too often, we don't tell someone how we feel because we fear the other person won't reciprocate or because we attach feelings of self-worth to others' responses. Sometimes we've lived so long without being vulnerable that it seems out of character to do so. But practicing vulnerability makes it easier to continue, and frequently when someone sees another person being vulnerable, they feel safe enough to be vulnerable as well.

Because of this, I try to tell my kids that I'm proud of them when I see them. My wife and I compliment each other often, and though sometimes the compliments are the same, it's always nice to hear how we perceive each other. I also make it a point to look my friends dead in the eyes and say, "Hey man, I really miss hanging out with you," or "I really value our friendship," or even "I'm really glad we're friends." How often do we say these things to those closest to us? I know I don't do it enough.

I don't have a lot of regrets in life because I've done many of the things I wanted to do, and even seemingly poor decisions led me to where I am. But one of my biggest regrets is that I never got to talk to my mentor, Tony, again before he passed away. It was one of those situations where we would message and talk about catching up, but he passed away before we did, and I can't undo that.

Remind those you love, "Hey, I'm still here." Choose them again and again. Take responsibility for your part of the relationship, especially when it's not going the way you want it to. Always be vulnerable with those who matter to you, and show others you appreciate them while they're here.

AUTHENTICITY

For genuine connection to occur, we must let go of who we believe we should be and instead be our authentic selves. Luckily, vulnerability naturally leads to authenticity.

Most people would like to be as authentic as possible, but it can be challenging when that desire is competing with the desire to be accepted by friends, family, or the world. For instance, you might go to a get-together thinking, "I'm not going to drink tonight," but when you walk in and someone hands you a drink, you take it—possibly out of habit. On another day, you might say, "I'm going to eat healthily," but then you join your friends who are all going out for pizza. You then find yourself making an excuse, "I ate well yesterday, so pizza won't hurt," or "I went to the gym today, so I guess I'll eat the pizza."

How do you know you're not being your authentic self? When you're pretending to be someone you're not or living in a way that seeks the approval of others.

Consider: are you chasing a career someone else wanted for you or working in the family business because that's what everyone before you did? Are you in a relationship or married because you're a certain age and that's "what you're supposed to do?" Maybe you learned a sport you can't stand to fit in with friends or coworkers. Perhaps you don't speak your mind in your relationship because you'd rather avoid an argument.

Unfortunately, these tendencies can lead to resentment, sadness, boredom, and anxiety, and you may even feel jealousy when you see someone living a life with no regrets. You can't be *your* Best Version Ever if you're not being *you*, after all.

Authenticity is about being yourself, not holding yourself back, and letting your light shine. It's about being considerate of others, but not to the detriment of yourself.

This transformation doesn't have to happen overnight, but when our friends, families, and the world know our true self—not the person we think we need to be or the person we think others want us to be—we can rest comfortably knowing that we are loved for who we are. It takes courage, but our most vital connections are made when we've opened up to others, experienced their empathy, and empathized with them in return.

TAKE ACTION

You are your most authentic self when there is no one to impress or conform to, so consider the following questions:

- Imagine your future self giving advice to your present self about living authentically. What would this person say to you? There are only two people in life that you want to impress: eighteen-year-old you and eighty-year-old you.
- What is one small step you could take toward being more authentic? For example, you might ask for something you want or speak up about something you usually wouldn't.

FORGIVENESS

On a few occasions, I have attended Alcoholics Anonymous (AA) meetings in support of a close friend. Once when I was there, a girl told the story of how she had written a letter apologizing to everyone she had hurt or let down in her life—but instead of sending that letter, she burned it. She then spoke about a future time when she could forgive herself.

Forgiveness is good for your body and mind, but getting there isn't easy; we hold grudges to protect ourselves from being harmed again the same way we were before. It can be tough to forgive someone who has hurt you or to forgive yourself for your mistakes, but holding on to grudges can drain us of energy, making us incapable of processing and resolving our problems.

Research shows that poor emotional regulation, the tendency to blame others, hiding emotions, and clinging to negative emotions all lead to more negative feelings, such as anxiety and depression. These tendencies can also negatively impact your body's stress hormone, cortisol, which can increase your heart rate, blood pressure, and weight gain.

In contrast, a study published in the *Annals of Behavioral Medicine* found that those who could forgive experienced a decrease in their perception of stress, leading to a reduction in psychological distress. Many studies have concluded that forgiveness can help victims overcome the adverse mental and physical effects of conflict.

However, you can't just say, "I forgive you," without experiencing sincere change. When you forgive, you consciously decide to let go of negative feelings, regardless of whether the person deserves it or not.

Often we are hesitant to initiate forgiveness because we expect the other person to apologize first after we've been wronged, but this rarely happens. Waiting for others to act first will usually lead to disappointment, so it's best if you take action. Your happiness shouldn't depend on anyone else.

We can be aware of the situations and behaviors in the past that have challenged our boundaries and contradicted our values without carrying grudges into our futures. Remember, we all make mistakes as humans.

When you consider the perspective of a person who has offended you, you may find common ground that leads to a deeper level of compassion and empathy. You can then take advantage of that understanding to change the situation right now. This is a necessary component of healing the pain of a lingering grudge.

As we learn to let go of hurt, anger, and resentment, we have the opportunity to realize positive insights, which may give us the closure we need to move on, move forward, and give back.

Learning to forgive takes practice, but it's worth it.

TAKE ACTION

Research has shown that writing about traumatic life events is associated with enhanced immune functioning and reduced health problems. So let's take a page out of the AA girl's book and write a forgiveness letter.

Write down everything you need to let go of. Who do you need to forgive, and what do you need forgiveness for? What are you holding on to that is holding you back from becoming your Best Version Ever? Let it all out. This letter is for your eyes only.

This is the part where I tell you to be safe: don't burn down the house, but light that letter on fire and watch it burn. If you're not comfortable burning the letter, then use a shredder. Then just let it all go.

GIVING BACK

Years ago, I had the chance to listen to Jeff Hoffman, who helped grow Priceline.com, and hear his story about realizing the power we all have to do more.

Jeff shared how one day while sitting at home alone, he saw a news story about a shelter for abused women that had run out of money. The shelter was closing, and women were crying as the owners were being evicted.

Jeff had an initial reaction, not unlike most of us: he didn't want to see that. *How depressing,* he thought. When the news anchor returned to say, "Coming up next, sports," Jeff felt a slight sense of relief.

As he flipped to another channel, he thought, *Man, they should help those women. They should do something.*

Then it hit him. He bolted out of his chair and wrote on the wall, "There is no 'they.'" Because if everyone watching the news report says "they" should do something, who does something? Nobody.

"They" do not exist; "we" do. "They" don't solve problems; "we" do.

Jeff called the news station, got information about the shelter, withdrew money from the bank, and dropped off cash in duffle bags…which was used to pay off the house so those women wouldn't be on the streets.

Most people want to impact others, but don't think they can make a significant enough difference or wait until they have "more money" or "more time." The truth is, you can do a little bit wherever you are in life, and you'll likely find that giving back is a natural step on your journey to becoming your Best Version Ever.

Listening to Jeff speak about his experience, I finally realized what *I* could do. I launched a local group that meets quarterly to raise money for charities. During our hour-long events, three nominated charities present, and the winning charity receives

$100 from each member. 100 members × $100 = $10,000 donation. Through small individual donations, we collectively make a huge impact.

LARGE-SCALE IMPACT

Sometimes people mistakenly say, "Money is the root of all evil." I say mistakenly because first, the saying is "The LOVE of money is the root of all evil," but second, they just haven't had the feeling you get when you give a lot of money away.

If someone thinks money is evil, it's because they haven't seen the good that can be done when money is directed to the right places. Money doesn't change people—it amplifies their character. If you're an asshole, money can make you an even bigger asshole; if you're a kind person, money can help you spread that kindness.

As you become your Best Version Ever, you may find you need to give back to continue growing. Giving back allows us to connect with a higher purpose, and it feels satisfying when we help others. Psychologists call this state of euphoria the "helper's high." When we give back, our bodies release endorphins, creating a feeling of general well-being. In other words, giving back benefits both the giver and the receiver.

When deciding how to give back, consider: what bothers me that needs to be fixed? Then, if you find yourself like Jeff Hoffman, asking why "they" aren't fixing something, you may already know what you could be supporting.

Once you've identified the cause(s) you're passionate about, research what is being done about it in your community. Here are some potential ways to make a large-scale impact:

- Participate in fundraisers and charity events
- Volunteer at a homeless shelter or a soup kitchen
- Volunteer at an animal shelter, hospital, nonprofit, or senior living community
- Volunteer with one of the ministries at your religious organization
- Donate blood
- Donate supplies to a school, a teacher, or kids in need
- Donate books to the library
- Find online stores that will donate a portion of the sales to charities you would like to support
- Pick up trash and plant trees in your community
- Pay it forward by paying for someone's coffee in line behind you, paying for someone's groceries, or paying for someone's gas
- Become a mentor with an organization like Boys & Girls Clubs of America and Big Brothers Big Sisters of America

If you don't see the thing you're searching for, maybe the world is asking you to create it. For instance, my friend Jon Vroman decided to make an impact by, as he puts it, marrying his greatest love with his greatest fear. Jon loves front row experiences and fears an illness cutting his life short, so he started Front Row Foundation, which provides world-class front row experiences like concerts and sporting events to those diagnosed with a terminal illness.

Maybe it's because I worked in a jail for five years, but my greatest fear has always been being wrongly convicted of a crime; my greatest love is helping others live extraordinary lives and become their Best Version Ever. So I've decided to donate a portion of all proceeds from this book to Innocence Project, a nonprofit that works to free the innocent, prevent wrongful convictions, and create fair, compassionate, and equitable systems of justice for everyone.

Whether you're supporting an organization or a neighbor, you can make a difference—and by buying this book, you already are.

ONE-TO-ONE IMPACT

One day, Jon was driving down the road when he came up to a toll booth. He handed $3 to the woman working in the booth, and as he handed her the money, she looked back at him, took the money, and said, "Hey sweetie, how are you doing?"

Jon looked back at her and said, as most of us would, "I'm good."

She looked back at Jon and yelled, "No!"

She paused. Two seconds, three seconds, then five seconds went by.

Jon didn't know what he had done wrong. What happened? How did he offend her?

She looked at him, grinned, threw one hand in the air, and yelled, "YOU… are SUPER FANTASTIC!"

Jon has never been able to forget that moment. He wondered, *Does she do this to every single car?*

Can you imagine, for eight hours, every single car, yelling, "YOU... are SUPER FANTASTIC!" How many times could a person do that?

Years later, Jon got an answer to his question while watching a McDonald's commercial. In the middle of the golden arches was the toll booth worker yelling, "Try it! It's SUPER FANTASTIC!"

Some people working in a toll booth may ask, "What difference can I make?" But, unfortunately, too often, we think like this:

"I just got hired—what difference can I make?"

"I'm an employee, not the manager—what difference can I make?"

"I'm the manager, but I don't own the company—what difference can I make?"

"I own the company, but I'm not the governor—what difference can I make?"

"I'm the governor, but I'm not the president—what difference can I make?"

This mentality goes on and on. It's easy to compare ourselves to others and feel our charitable contributions will never make a difference. It's easy to see others giving more and feel like you can't make a difference.

But impact is not a competition. Every little bit helps; every little bit matters. The woman in the toll booth knew that even her simple one-on-one interaction could make a difference in people's lives.

Consider the kind of impact you can make with even a single person. Your impact might be becoming a mentor. It might be:

- Letting a friend stay at your house when they're having a rough time
- Stopping to help someone pulled over on the side of the road
- Mowing your neighbor's lawn and bringing in your neighbor's trash cans
- Adding a loving note to your kids' or significant other's lunch
- Teaching someone a new skill
- Over-tipping your server
- Giving someone a gift for no reason
- Sending someone a handwritten note of gratitude
- Making sandwiches and passing them out to those in need
- Doing housework and maintenance for your elderly neighbor
- Sharing a friendly smile or saying "hello" to someone you walk by on the sidewalk

These random acts of kindness for even a single person can go a long way.

MOVING FORWARD

While vacationing in a coastal village, an entrepreneur watched a small boat dock with just one fisherman. The boat contained several large, fresh fish.

The entrepreneur was impressed with the size of the fish and asked the fisherman how long it took to catch them.

"Only a couple of hours," he replied. When the entrepreneur asked why he didn't stay out longer, the fisherman explained that his small catch was more than enough to cover his family's needs.

"And what do you do with the rest of your time?" the entrepreneur asked.

"I sleep late, fish a little, play with my kids, have lunch with my wife, and stroll into the village each evening to play guitar with friends. I live a full life."

The entrepreneur said, "I've got an Ivy League MBA, and I can help you. The first thing you should do is fish longer every day. Then you can sell the extra fish you catch. With the extra money, you can buy a bigger boat. With the extra money the larger boat will bring, you can buy a second and a third one, and so on until you have a large fleet. Then, instead of selling your fish to a middleman, you can negotiate directly with the processing plants or open your own. From there, you can run your huge corporation from a big city here or even in the United States."

"But how long will that take?" asked the fisherman.

"Oh, fifteen, maybe twenty years."

"Then what?"

"That's the best part," the entrepreneur laughed. "When the time's right, you can sell shares of stock in your company and make millions."

"Millions? Then what?"

"Then you would retire. You could move to a small coastal village where you could sleep late, fish a little, play with your kids, have lunch with your wife, and stroll into the village each evening to play guitar with friends."

The fisherman smiled and shook his head.

The point of becoming your Best Version Ever isn't to grind until you can't anymore—it's to build the life you want while loving the life you have. In the process, you may find that you no longer hold yourself back or aim low to avoid the criticism of the crowd. You may not be interested in the menial things you used to do. You may not want to stay up late getting drunk. You may live counter to others' expectations, and you may even run the risk that your friends will say, "You've changed."

If so, good job.

You've worked on your mindset, aim, gameplan, immersion, and consistency. You've worked on refocusing, connecting, and giving back. You have and are continuing to evolve. You shouldn't apologize for being awesome.

The more you become your Best Version Ever, the more you show others the life that's possible for all of us. The more you show them what's possible, the more it shines a light on what they're not doing. Some will resent your success, but most will cheer you on. So throw down the rope; help them scale mountains with you.

Give yourself permission to be your Best Version Ever, regardless of what others think. Give yourself permission to rest and start over when you need to. We can impact the world just by becoming the most extraordinary versions of ourselves.

CONCLUSION

Best Version Ever has been a work in progress for at least seven years.

I initially thought I would write a book about changing your business—and the world—by differentiating yourself as a real estate agent. That makes sense, right? Real estate has been my career for almost half my life. I even ran the idea by a bestselling author and entrepreneur, who encouraged me to go for it.

I may still write that book, but as I started the writing process, I realized I wanted to write a book that could help anyone, not just real estate agents.

I spent my entire twenties working at a jail to support my family, only to realize I was exhausted and barely saw my kids. I spent my thirties building my real estate business, only to realize I didn't want my identity to revolve around my career. When I turned thirty-eight, I thought, *If you were to die today, what would they say about you? Would they say that you were a good real estate agent?*

I realized I wanted to be remembered as someone who gives back and inspires others. I wanted to write a book that my kids, my niece, my goddaughter, or any family member could pick up, even twenty years from now, and be able to learn and grow from.

This realization coincided perfectly with me opening up my goal planning event to the public, where I had guests from various industries attend and take life-changing actions for the first time. I suddenly understood that becoming *my* Best Version Ever involved using my MAGIC formula to impact the world around me.

To do this, I changed my mindset about writing books. I reflected on the book I had written several years ago, which was more like a marketing tool to gain clients, and reflected on the kind of book I wanted to write this time. I saw friends publish life-changing, bestselling books and knew I could do it myself.

I then determined my aim. I set specific intentions for my book, like publishing this year and donating a portion of the proceeds to charity. I visualized what my book would say and what it would mean to have written it—the impact it would have on others' lives and my own.

Afterward, I created a gameplan, from taking the initial action of hiring a publishing team to developing and implementing a consistent writing plan. Instead of staring mindlessly at a screen for hours every day, I scheduled regular calls with the team, working on writing, editing, revisions, proofreading, layout, marketing, and more.

As I developed my gameplan, I also researched ways to immerse myself in publishing. Besides finding the team I wanted to work with, I reaffirmed my commitment and read a few books and articles on the publishing process. I also reached out to people who could mentor me, and asked for presales, reviews, and promotion opportunities.

Finally, I stuck to my gameplan by setting aside time to write every week, even on vacation. I got rid of distractions during my writing time, tracked my progress, and wouldn't let myself do anything else until I had completed my writing for the day.

If I can do this, you can too. Just ask yourself, *What does my Best Version Ever look like right now? Who do I need to become to achieve my goals?* Then, remember and implement the MAGIC formula:

- **Mindset:** Shift your thinking from negative to positive so that you can control how you react to situations and respond to opportunities.
- **Aim:** Determine who you want to be and the goals that will help you become that person, knowing that those goals may change as you grow.
- **Gameplan:** Develop checklists and schedules for your short- and long-term goals and take immediate action to gain momentum.
- **Immersion:** Find ways to regularly learn and challenge yourself to get past plateaus in your progress.
- **Consistency:** Build the environment and the habits that set you up for sustained success—and track them to see growth and areas requiring improvement.

Becoming your Best Version Ever requires intentionality and

massive action. It requires you to be authentic and vulnerable, and give yourself grace when you face setbacks. It requires you to embrace change, knowing that you will evolve, and so will your vision for your life. And when you can't grow anymore serving yourself, becoming your Best Version Ever requires you to consider how your talents can serve the world around you.

That's where the MAGIC happens.

You can connect with Josh and find
additional resources to become your Best
Version Ever at BestVersionEver.com

ACKNOWLEDGMENTS

To my beautiful wife, Courtney: You sacrificed the most during this book writing process, holding things down and allowing me the space I needed. Thank you so much for the feedback and support…I love you so much.

To the inspiration for this book: Andrew Painter, Chloe Painter, Samantha Higgins, and Presley Sellers. I love you all and hope this helps in years to come.

To everyone on my publishing and launch team: Huge thanks to my editor, Kathleen McIntosh, who put up with my nonstop changes and questions and helped put everything I was thinking onto paper. I couldn't have done it without you. To Barbara Boyd for the second set of eyes and great insight, Eliece Pool for putting the band together, Mario Vargas for photography, and Michael Nagin for the best book cover I could have ever imagined. To Amber Vilhauer, Alexis Snell, and Megan O'Malley: thank you so much for seeing the vision and taking the time to get everything just perfect.

To my parents: Your experiences and lives made me who I am today, and I wouldn't change a thing. 1 in 400 trillion. To my mother-in-law, Jeannine: I always say you're the best mother-in-law I've ever had.

To my siblings: My brother, Chris, and sister-in-law, Alissa: thank you both for all your support, and you're both too far away from everyone.

To my friends and framily: Patrick Sellers, Christy Sellers, Presley Sellers, Annette Sagastume, Shauna Guesman, Jason Guesman, Shelly Rusk-Olivieri, Stacey Rusk-Olivieri, Jeff Borbolla, April Arechiga, Kari Dukerschein, Alina Jefferies, Neva Calderon, Bubba Ferguson, Natalie Ferguson, Sean Foley, Mick Wilson, Ashlyn Wilson, Ed Ulufanua, Carla Ulufanua, Michelle Barney, Randy Sabbara, Lindy Sabbara (aka Best Neighbors Ever, aka #TeamPS Starpoint Crew). Justin Grable, Jarmila Grable, Greg Amoroso, Ryan McCulloch, Jay Hitz, John Baker, Tommy Powell, Jill Powell, Dennis Irwin, Adriana Irwin, Jarrett Johnson, Shannon Johnson, Frank Romo, Nick Murray, Ryan McCray, Alex McCray, Steve DeSena, Garrett Brookman, Karen Brookman, Sal Correa, Liv Scarry, Lynn Gardipee, Lindsay Ciota, Bonnie Nieves, Brandy Markakis, Josh Wilkinson, Carlos Checo, Kelly Gilson, Dani Gilson, Niki Rhodes, Jim Frageau, Kristen Gabel, Joe Galante, Anthony Morel, Rosa Vargas, Nikki Antibus, Blake Mayer, Philip Thomas, Joannie Alvarez, Shishana Hogg, Cortney Shurtleff, Marshall Parsons, Kristen Jewell, Brad Brenkus, Rick Hanson, Aldo Hernandez.

To my OG accountability crew for the support and feedback along the way: Scott Groves, Ernest Hernandez, Mario Mazzamuto, Mark Walker.

To my SoCal accountability crew for the support and feedback along the way: Joseph Arendsen, Christian Ballow, Billy Bell, Brian Bender, Mark Berns, Jay Bourgana, John Ceisel, Dasean Cunningham, Kenneth Donaghy, Tom Donnelly, Matt Floyd, Kelly Gilson, Greg Kaseno, Gody Khambatta, Kevin McGrath, John McPherson, Aleks Memca, Brian Moore, Rob Roswell, Jeremy Taylor, Joshua Thacker, Doug Spence, Tri Vu, Rob Wolfe.

To my mentors: I've been fortunate enough to have so many along the way, some I've known and some I'll never meet. I can never thank you enough. Tony Sisca, Tim Braheem, Hal Elrod, Jon Vroman, Jon Berghoff, John Kitchin, Bill Madigan, Elijah Scott, Mark Bender, Mark Sisson, Jared Falk, Dave Atkinson, Mike Michalkow, Mike Johnston, Darren Hardy, Tony Robbins, Matthew Kelly, Neale Donald Walsch, Howard Zinn, Michael Singer, Eddie Vedder, Randy Cooke, Matt Cameron, Shannon Larkin.

To friends I've created music with: Frank Romo, Nick Murray, Ryan McCray, Alex McCray, Steve DeSena, Mark Bender, Shred Sean Maier, Andrew Deck, Catherine Deck, Jonathan Shelley, PJ Chesney, Shawn Sullivan, Michael Lundin.

To everyone who trusted in Best Version Ever Live, before it was a thing: Steve DeSena, Lynn Gardipee, Garrett Brookman, Karen Brookman, Lindsay Ciota, Carlos Checo, Sal Correa, Niki Rhodes, Lisa Barba, Merav Shina, Guadalupe Belandres, Annet Nakamoto, Edward Philbrick, Ivy Tsai, Barbie Blackmore, Tom Tucker, Ashley Thomas, Janet Rabbia, Jody Heckel, Vanessa Clifford, Cliff Clifford, Jim Frageau, Nikki Antibus, Rosa Vargas, David Butler, Julie Butler, Bonnie Nieves, Christine Sabalza, Sally Stovall, Liza Gomez, Ariel Druck, Jeff Perez, Rob Wolfe,

Lynsey Genin, Nicole Johnson, Matt Johnson, Jay Greene, Marcy Sattelmaier, Kyle Niemi, Kenneth Donaghy, Greg Amoroso, Mia Flores, Tri Vu, Quynh Vu, Cathie Kong, Aly Kong, Shishana Hogg, Wafaa Barajas, Carlie Bernstein, Kim Van Sickle, Chase Penrose, Lori Steegmans, Charmaine Orcino-Gonzales.

To everyone who trusted in Temecula's Impact Club: Steve DeSena (the first member), Ryan McCulloch, Justin Grable, Kristen Gabel, Kellie Tuer (thank you for your sponsorships!), Mike Ackley, Ashley Aguilera, Matt Alexander, Rob Alvarez, Greg Amoroso, Nikki Arango, Bobby Archuleta, Lisa Archuleta, Amanda Ballow, Deborah Beach, Rebekah Bigelow, Lindsay Blue, Natalie Bocanegra, Kate Botterell, Adam Bouvet, Brad Brenkus, Debbie Breslin, Garrett Brookman, Karen Brookman, Tonya Broussard, Jeannine Brown, David Browne, Sean Burgess, Betsy Burkey, Amanda Burns, Windy Busher, John Butler, Bob Cadez, Anne Callahan, Guy Campbell, Heather Chance, Carlos Checo, Jill Chrapczynski, Lindsay Ciota, Windy Ciucki, Marie Clark, Regina Clark, Caroline Claypool, Elizabeth Clements, Gina Colonna, Ashley Cooper, Eliu Cordova, Veronica Cordova, Sal Correa, Sarah Crane, Travis Crow, Rebecca Dahl, Christian Dahlin, Joe Daquino, Karen Davis, Matthew Davis, Aaron Dean, Ashley DeBoer, Brian Decker, Alison Decker, Eddie De La Rosa, Timothy Delmundo, Lisa De Ritis, Angelica Diaz, Jenny Di Bernardo, Grattan Donahoe, Jenna Drawe, Jennifer Duregger, Gena Elfelt, Darcee Ellefson, Deano Esades, Elizabeth Falvey, Robert Fanzo, Scott Farnam, Ryan Fletcher, Lisa Forss, Deanna Fox, Adam Fuller, Chris Gabel, Joe Galante, Neal Gann, Nicole Gann, Tracey Garamone, Lynn Gardipee, Ryan Garland, Kara Garland, Jenna Garza, Andrew Gavin, Sharon Geier, Kelly Gilson, Dani Gilson, Tammy Golden, Beth Good, Stacey Griffin, Jamie Grijalva, Scott Groves, Jon Gwin, Xiomara

Hall, Alicia Ham, Pam Harris, Alonna Hauser, Jeremy Hauser, Bob Hellman, Ivonne Hemmer, Erika Hessler, Keith Hicks, Michelle Hinkley, Jay Hitz, Hudson Hogg, Shishana Hogg, Todd Holland, Dennis Irwin, Adriana Irwin, Bill Jawitz, Jason Jernigan, Charlie Johnson IV, Jeremy Joyce, Kevin Kansaki, Dan Keck, Lauren Kline, Scott Koth, Adam Kutchuk, Danielle Lane, Tony Langdon, Kathy Lansford, Karen La Pointe, Kimberly Legg, Jaclyn Leizerowicz, Joshua Lent, Pete Lent, Molly Le Vine, Beth Lichtenberger, Marci Lipp, Jennifer Lorek, Tobie Love, Michael Luna, Brandy Markakis, George Markakis, Christina Martin, Debbie Martis, Brittany Marvin, Blake Mayer, Shawn McDonald, Sally McDonald, Jennifer McDonald, Todd McGregor, Kevin McGrew, Mark McLeavy, Dave Medina, Kim Meeker, Linda Mejia, Kelly Messick, Jonathan Mezzadri, Shelly Milison, Laurel Miller, George Mills, Jodi Mills, Kambria Minton, Nancy Mireles, Ben Mireles, Shelly Moore, Vern Moter, Connie Murphy, Rebecca Neeley, David Neugart, Sokha Ngov, Tacy Nichols, Brittany Nicola, Chris Niesen, Jason O'Brien, Frank O'Connor, Caroline Ollison, Joseph Onello, Bill Owen, Jerri Owen, Kim Owens, Micheal Parrish, Sean Parsons, Christopher Payne, Silvia Pena, Rich Pflugradt, Sharon Pflugradt, Peggy Pinto, Adria Pointdexter, Tommy Powell, Jill Powell, Chad Power, Sarah Power, John Powers, David Pyle, Nicole Racz, Sara Ramsey, Vail Raymer, Angel Reza, Steve Ribultan, Jennifer Richard, Ryan Rinderspacher, Summer Rinderspacher, Shahla Rivera, Brandon Roberts, Kelly Robertson, Ryan Rogers, Elizabeth Roth, Tiffany Romero, Regina Rovere, Vanessa Ruelas, John Ruff, Steven Russell, Traci Russell, Randy Sabbara, Lindy Sabbara, Greg Schacher, MaryAnn Sharp, David Shaw, Vickie Shaw, Jillian Sidoti, Katerina Sikova, Ang Sillin, Cathy Sine, Patty Smith, Jon Solek, Trichelle Solomon, Matt Soper, Austin Sorensen, Shawn Sorensen, Ryan Steinbuch, Valen Steinbuch,

James "Stew" Stewart, Magda Stewart, Toni Stone, Rachel Strickland, Steve Swanson, Evan Taylor, Jeremy Taylor, Steve Tempel, Autumn Termine, Philip Thomas, Sherry Thompson, Mary Thompson, Jennifer Todd, Karen Totty, Kristine Turner, Charles Vamadeva, Frank Van Dyke, Steve Van Houten, Mario Vargas, Daniel Vasquez, Chris Veloz, Lori Wakatake, Michael Wall, Cindy Warren, Chris Waterman, Cari Wear, Mike Weber, Kathy Weber, Robert Wells, Greg Wick, Josh Wilkinson, Susan Williams, George Williams, Alan Winkelstein, Pauline Woelky, Robyn Wonnell, Denise Wood, Michele Wyckoff.

BIBLIOGRAPHY

Akhtar, Sadaf, Alan Dolan, and Jane Barlow. "Understanding the Relationship between State Forgiveness and Psychological Wellbeing: A Qualitative Study." *Journal of Religion and Health* 56, no. 2 (April 2017): 450–463. https://doi.org/10.1007/s10943-016-0188-9.

Avildsen, John G., dir. *The Karate Kid*. Culver City, CA: Columbia Pictures, 1984.

Choi, Eun-Ha. *Crash Factors in Intersection-Related Crashes: An on-Scene Perspective: Report Number DOT HS 811 366*. Washington, DC: NHTSA's National Center for Statistics and Analysis, September 2010. https://crashstats.nhtsa.dot.gov/Api/Public/ViewPublication/811366.

Clear, James. "Why Trying to Be Perfect Won't Help You Achieve Your Goals (and What Will)." *James Clear* (blog). Accessed September 7, 2022. https://jamesclear.com/repetitions.

Comaford, Christine. "I Stalked Steve Jobs (and How to Get a Meeting with Any VIP)." *Forbes*, November 10, 2011. https://www.forbes.com/sites/christinecomaford/2011/11/10/i-stalked-steve-jobs-and-how-to-get-a-meeting-with-any-vip.

Compare, Angelo, Cristina Zarbo, Edo Shonin, William Van Gordon, and Chiara Marconi. "Emotional Regulation and Depression: A Potential Mediator between Heart and Mind." *Cardiovascular Psychiatry and Neurology* 2014 (June 2014): 324374. https://doi.org/10.1155/2014/324374.

Dumas, John Lee. *The Common Path to Uncommon Success: A Roadmap to Financial Freedom and Fulfillment.* New York: HarperCollins Leadership, 2021.

Ghosh, Rajashi, and Thomas G. Reio Jr. "Career Benefits Associated with Mentoring for Mentors: A Meta-Analysis." *Journal of Vocational Behavior* 83, no. 1 (August 2013): 106–116. https://doi.org/10.1016/j.jvb.2013.03.011.

Goodman, Joshua, Michael Hurwitz, Jisung Park, and Jonathan Smith. "Heat and Learning." National Bureau of Economic Research Working Paper 24639, Cambridge, MA, May 2018, revised November 2019. https://doi.org/10.3386/w24639.

Harvard Health Publishing. "Blue Light Has a Dark Side: What Is Blue Light? The Effect Blue Light Has on Your Sleep and More." *Harvard Health Blog*, July 7, 2020. https://www.health.harvard.edu/staying-healthy/blue-light-has-a-dark-side.

Harvard Medical School. "Harvard Second Generation Study." Accessed August 28, 2022. https://www.adultdevelopmentstudy.org/.

Invitation Digital. "How Many Productive Hours in a Work Day? Just 2 Hours, 23 Minutes…" Vouchercloud. Accessed August 27, 2022. https://www.vouchercloud.com/resources/office-worker-productivity.

Izenberg, Josh. "Slomo." *New York Times*, March 31, 2014. https://www.nytimes.com/2014/04/01/opinion/slomo.html.

Koselka, Elizabeth P. D., Lucy C. Weidner, Arseniy Minasov, Marc G. Berman, William R. Leonard, Marianne V. Santoso, Junia N. de Brito, Zachary C. Pope, Mark A. Pereira, and Teresa H. Horton. "Walking Green: Developing an Evidence Base for Nature Prescriptions." *International Journal of Environmental Research and Public Health* 16, no. 22 (November 2019): 4338. https://doi.org/10.3390/ijerph16224338.

Lang, Susan S. "It's the Size of the Meal, Not the Size of the Person, That Determines How People Underestimate Calories, Cornell Study Finds." *Cornell Chronicle*, November 1, 2006. https://news.cornell.edu/stories/2006/11/bigger-meal-more-we-underestimate-its-calories.

Langer, Ellen J. *Counter Clockwise: Mindful Health and the Power of Possibility*. New York: Ballantine Books, 2009.

Locke, Edwin A., Karyll N. Shaw, Lise M. Saari, and Gary P. Latham. "Goal Setting and Task Performance: 1969–1980." *Psychological Bulletin* 90, no. 1 (1981): 125–152. https://doi.org/10.1037/0033-2909.90.1.125.

Murray, Bridget. "Writing to Heal." *Monitor on Psychology* 33, no. 6 (June 2002): 54. https://www.apa.org/monitor/jun02/writing.

Nevada Sales Agency. "Light Bulb! Discover How Lighting Affects Productivity." December 17, 2019. http://www.nevadasalesagency.com/2019/12/17/light-bulb-discover-how-lighting-affects-productivity/.

Olivet Nazarene University. "Study Explores Professional Mentor–Mentee Relationships in 2019." Accessed September 6, 2022. https://online.olivet.edu/research-statistics-on-professional-mentors.

Pond, Meredith. "6 Ways to Block Fluorescent Lights at Work—and 1 Way Not To." Axon Optics, July 15, 2022. https://www.axonoptics.com/6-ways-to-block-fluorescent-lights-at-work-and-1-way-not-to/.

Prisco, Jacopo, and Anastasia Beltyukova. "Why UPS Trucks (Almost) Never Turn Left." *CNN*, February 23, 2017. https://www.cnn.com/2017/02/16/world/ups-trucks-no-left-turns.

Quan, Stuart F., ed. "Twelve Simple Tips to Improve Your Sleep." Healthy Sleep. Last modified December 18, 2007. https://healthysleep.med.harvard.edu/healthy/getting/overcoming/tips.

Ranganathan, Vinoth K., Vlodek Siemionow, Jing Z. Liu, Vinod Sahgal, and Guang H. Yue. "From Mental Power to Muscle Power—Gaining Strength by Using the Mind." *Neuropsychologia* 42, no. 7 (2004): 944–956. https://doi.org/10.1016/j.neuropsychologia.2003.11.018.

Raypole, Crystal. "Music and Studying: It's Complicated." Healthline. Laste updated June 22, 2022. https://www.healthline.com/health/does-music-help-you-study.

Schultz, Howard, and Joanne Gordon. *Onward: How Starbucks Fought for Its Life without Losing Its Soul.* New York: Rodale, 2011.

Sridharan, Devarajan, Daniel J. Levitin, Chris H. Chafe, Jonathan Berger, and Vinod Menon. "Neural Dynamics of Event Segmentation in Music: Converging Evidence for Dissociable Ventral and Dorsal Networks." *Neuron* 50, no. 3 (August 2007): 521–532. https://doi.org/10.1016/j.neuron.2007.07.003.

Toussaint, Loren L., Grant S. Shields, and George M. Slavich. "Forgiveness, Stress, and Health: A 5-Week Dynamic Parallel Process Study." *Annals of Behavioral Medicine* 50, no. 5 (October 2016): 727–735. https://doi.org/10.1007/s12160-016-9796-6.

Turakitwanakan, Wanpen, Chantana Mekseepralard, and Panaree Busarakumtragul. "Effects of Mindfulness Meditation on Serum Cortisol of Medical Students." *Journal of the Medical Association of Thailand = Chotmaihet Thangphaet* 96, no. Suppl 1 (2013): S90–S95. https://pubmed.ncbi.nlm.nih.gov/23724462/.

Ware, Bronnie. *The Top Five Regrets of the Dying: A Life Transformed by the Dearly Departing.* Carlsbad, CA: Hay House, 2011.

Weingarten, Gene. "Pearls before Breakfast: Can One of the Nation's Great Musicians Cut through the Fog of a D.C. Rush Hour? Let's Find Out." *Washington Post*, April 8, 2007. https://www.washingtonpost.com/lifestyle/magazine/pearls-before-breakfast-can-one-of-the-nations-great-musicians-cut-through-the-fog-of-a-dc-rush-hour-lets-find-out/2014/09/23/8a6d46da-4331-11e4-b47c-f5889e061e5f_story.html.

Wikipedia. s.v. "Roger Bannister." Last modified August 31, 2022, 06:38. https://en.wikipedia.org/wiki/Roger_Bannister.

Wilkins, Arnold J., Ian Nimmo-Smith, A. I. Slater, and L. Bedocs. "Fluorescent Lighting, Headaches and Eyestrain." *Lighting Research and Technology* 21, no. 1 (March 1989): 11–18. https://doi. org/10.1177/096032718902100102.

Winfrey, Orpah, and Jim Carrey. *Oprah's Life Class.* "What Oprah Learned from Jim Carrey." Aired October 12, 2011, on OWN. https://www.oprah. com/oprahs-lifeclass/what-oprah-learned-from-jim-carrey-video.

Zhang, Maggie. "The Founder of FedEx Saved the Company from Bankruptcy with His Blackjack Winnings." *Business Insider*, July 16, 2014. https://www.businessinsider.com/ fedex-saved-from-bankruptcy-with-blackjack-winnings-2014-7.

ABOUT THE AUTHOR

JOSH PAINTER is a husband, father, leader, coach, speaker, philanthropist, and the author of the book *Best Version Ever*.

Josh founded the Best Version Ever Community after realizing that most people live a life that others expect of them, not a life true to themselves. Unfortunately, he lived this same life, moving from one job to the next, barely getting by, and at one point almost losing everything.

Since then, Josh has built and sold a successful real estate company, started a charity organization, and lives his Best Version Ever by helping others crush their goals and reach their full potential in all areas of life.

CPSIA information can be obtained
at www.ICGtesting.com
Printed in the USA
BVHW052303201122
652392BV00003B/130